50 WELLBEING LESSONS FOR THE DIVERSE PRIMARY CLASSROOM

This book is designed to support teachers in promoting social and emotional wellbeing within their diverse classroom. With 50 detailed lessons plans and supplemented resources to promote discussion, each lesson plan contains learning outcomes, activity descriptions and further questions around areas of diversity specific to race, culture and LGBTQ+.

This accessible text offers a collection of activities with supplemented resources on a wide range of pertinent topics that challenge children to reflect, ask questions, analyse and find solutions through open discussion and collaboration. It provides them with the opportunity to explore their feelings and understand empathy and develop coping strategies in order to promote mental wellbeing. The content covered in this resource includes topics such as the psychological impact of discrimination, the Black Lives Matter movement, prejudice, coping with loss, feeling left out, moving school and managing as a young carer.

A practical guide ideal for those new to teaching as well as more experienced practitioners, this resource will help address social and emotional wellbeing through themes that often affect marginalised groups and is crucial reading for anyone looking to embed an inclusive mental wellbeing culture within their school.

Manisha Tailor, MBE is an experienced primary school practitioner and former Deputy Headteacher. She is company director of Swaggarlicious Ltd where she provides mental health and diversity education and works full time at a professional football club overseeing coaching. She also works for Show Racism the Red Card and The FA delivering Equality Education.

'This text will be a great resource for teachers in highlighting the importance of mental health and emotional well-being. It also offers guidance on case scenarios that can help prevent events happening and ways in dealing with them at a practical level. A greater in-depth questioning and self-reflection identifies the impact this has on children's learning and development with a positive outcome.'

Mr Umesh Raja, Headteacher (The Swaminarayan Preparatory School).

'Manisha has worked for Show Racism the Red Card now since 2014 and is one of our most skilled and knowledgeable educators of young people. She has delivered equalities training in a wide range of settings, including schools within Inner London and those in less diverse areas of the UK. Manisha has also successfully delivered workshops for SRtRC overseas and is a greatly respected member of our Team. More recently Manisha has led the development of workshops and resources which help young people improve their emotional wellbeing. Some of the exercises from those workshops are included in this publication and I am positive they will be of great use to all teachers working with young people of all ages.'

Steve Goodsell, Southern Regional Manager (Show Racism the Red Card).

'Manisha Tailor MBE has been an active changemaker within the sport and physical activity sector striving continually for diversity and equality for sport and mental health with a plethora of very impactful projects. Being the Vice-Chair for Coaching in Sporting Equals' British Asians in Sport and Physical Activity (BASPA) Advisory Board, we know she has the experience, sensitivity and knowledge to share best practice for mental health, wellbeing, diversity and inclusion. We are sure that those who access this guide will gain so much value and insight – leading to an increase in empathy and awareness.'

Arun Kang OBE, CEO Sporting Equals.

50 WELLBEING LESSONS FOR THE DIVERSE PRIMARY CLASSROOM

TEACHING THROUGH INCLUSIVE PRACTICE

Manisha Tailor

Illustrated by
Radhika Tailor

Routledge
Taylor & Francis Group

LONDON AND NEW YORK

First published 2021
by Routledge
2 Park Square, Milton Park, Abingdon, Oxon OX14 4RN

and by Routledge
52 Vanderbilt Avenue, New York, NY 10017

Routledge is an imprint of the Taylor & Francis Group, an informa business

British Library Cataloguing-in-Publication Data
A catalogue record for this book is available from the British Library

Library of Congress Cataloging-in-Publication Data
A catalog record has been requested for this book

ISBN: 978-0-367-70826-9 (hbk)
ISBN: 978-0-367-70825-2 (pbk)
ISBN: 978-1-003-14816-6 (ebk)

Typeset in DIN pro
by Deanta Global Publishing, Services, Chennai, India

CONTENTS

Contents

Contents

Contents

ABOUT THE AUTHOR

Manisha Tailor MBE is an experienced primary school practitioner and former Deputy Headteacher. She has extensive experience of working in diverse settings across the UK. Her journey of becoming a young carer for her twin brother who suffered from a mental health breakdown due to bullying, along with her passion for football and education, became her inspiration in creating *50 Wellbeing Lessons for the Diverse Primary Classroom: Teaching Through Inclusive Practice*.

> No child or young person deserves to be bullied or treated unfairly and be made to feel so isolated that they are fearful of speaking out.

> No child or young person should have to cope with becoming a young carer on their own or feel ashamed in talking about mental health.

> *50 Wellbeing Lessons for the Diverse Primary Classroom: Teaching Through Inclusive Practice* is for all those who have a duty of care and commitment to the welfare and safety of children. It is for those who have a responsibility in ensuring mental health and wellbeing is at the heart of school ethos and culture.

> Together let us create "Champions for Change" by creating open discussion on topics that matter to the children and educating them on topics that will help them to develop as learners for life. It is time to change the face of mental health in schools and our wider society through inclusive practice.

> **Manisha Tailor MBE**

FOREWORD

In an increasingly fast-paced world, understanding mental health and wellbeing has never been more important. As the modern world demands more of our attention, we become disconnected from our own needs and happiness, leading to a population where anxiety, depression and other mental health issues are common.

Mental health problems affect about 1 in 10 children and young people. Alarmingly, however, 70% of children and young people who experience a mental health problem have not had appropriate interventions at a sufficiently early age, and with 75% of mental health problems in adult life (excluding dementia) starting by the age of 18, it's clear that the sooner we begin to spot signs in childhood and provide the necessary support, the better.

Our emotional wellbeing is just as important as our physical health and whilst much work has been done by a range of agencies to raise awareness and understanding about this, much more needs to be done in schools.

We should not underestimate the extent and long term impact of poor mental health in children and young people:

- 75% of adults with a diagnosable mental health problem experience the first symptoms by the age of 24 (Kessler et al., 2005; McGorry et al., 2007).

- Severe and persistent behavioural problems starting before secondary school years which go unsupported can have long term impact on children's mental health and life chances (Brown et al., 2012).

- The most common mental health problem affecting children are conduct disorders (severe and persistent behavioural problems). These problems are around twice as likely to be experienced by boys/young men than girls/young women (Green et al., 2005).

- 5% children aged 5–10 have conduct disorder; this increases to 7% as young people approach secondary school years (Green et al., 2005).

- Children from low-income families are 4 times more likely to experience mental health problems than children from higher-income families (Morrison Gutman et al., 2015).

Whilst three-quarters of parents of children who are unwell seek help (mostly from schools) only one-quarter of children receive any support (Green et al., 2005).

"Mental health" was not in my vocabulary as a youngster, but it is slowly coming into the minds of students, parents and teachers today. My experience of working in mental health for over 10 years tells me that children and young people cannot flourish in the school environment unless their self-esteem and readiness to learn are carefully nurtured by skilled teachers and support staff.

Good mental health allows children and young people to develop the resilience to cope with whatever life throws at them and grow into well-rounded, healthy adults – that's why at The Kaleidoscope Plus Group, we believe that emotional wellbeing should form part of the national curriculum.

The delivery of effective services clearly hinges upon the many NHS and voluntary sector partners involved. Yet it is teachers that are de facto in the front-line when it comes to identifying and nurturing children's emotional wellbeing. Hence the need also for mental health training to be part of in-service provision for teachers. We also need to see a trained lead for mental health and wellbeing in every school and ensure that young people are involved in designing in-school bespoke support.

With the number and type of mental health issues in children and young people on the rise, and as more and more teachers are being pushed to the front lines of defence, there is a greater need for a comprehensive, practical resource that guides professionals through the complexities of child and adolescent mental health. This practical, comprehensive resource, expertly written by Manisha Tailor MBE, answers that call.

This book lays out an intuitive and practical approach to mental health and wellbeing that any school can adopt to transform their mental health support for students. With a focus on providing staff with practical tools on a limited budget, it helps schools make a real difference to student mental health. It sets out a roadmap for staff to create robust mental health support for students without requiring specific qualifications in this area of work and helps to embed mental health at the heart of the school's philosophy.

Monica Shafaq
CEO – The Kaleidoscope Plus Group

References

Brown, E.R., Khan, L. and Parsonage, M. (2012) *A chance to change: Delivering effective parenting programmes to transform lives*. London: Centre for Mental Health.

Green, H. et al. (2005) *The mental health of children and young people in Great Britain 2004*. Basingstoke: Palgrave.

Kessler, R.C. et al. (2005) Lifetime prevalence and age-at-onset distributions of DSM-IV disorders in the National Comorbidity Survey Replication. *Archives of General Psychiatry*, 62, pp. 593–602.

McGorry, P.D., Purcell, R., Hickie, I.B. and Jorm, A.F. (2007) Investing in youth mental health is a best buy. *Medical Journal of Australia*, 187(7), pp. 5–7.

Morrison Gutman, L., Joshi, H., Parsonage, M. and Schoon, I. (2015) *Children of the new century: Mental health findings from the Millenium Cohort Study*. London: Centre for Mental Health. www.centreforme ntalhealth.org.uk/sites/default/files/2018-09/CentreforMentalHealth_ChildrenYoungPeople_Fa ctsheet.pdf   Accessed 6/10/2020.

WHY TEACH ABOUT MENTAL HEALTH IN PRIMARY SCHOOLS?

Learning about mental health must be developmental, and for young children, rehearsing ways of asking an adult for help, persevering and showing resilience if they find something difficult, lays the foundations for confidently accessing sources of support when they are older.

50 Wellbeing Lessons for the Diverse Primary Classroom: Teaching Through Inclusive Practice is a resource aimed at supporting teachers to promote mental health through an introduction of a broad and diverse curriculum. The teaching activities can be used as a tool for providing children with opportunities to explore feelings, empathy, growth mindset and develop coping strategies as well as ways of keeping themselves healthy and safe.

50 Wellbeing Lessons for the Diverse Primary Classroom: Teaching Through Inclusive Practice offers a collection of activities with supplemented resources on a wide range of pertinent topics that challenges children to reflect, ask questions, analyse and find solutions through open discussion and collaboration. Talking openly and honestly with children about mental health issues is a simple and effective way of breaking down any possible associated stigma.

Before teaching about mental health and emotional wellbeing, it is important to establish clear ground rules to help create and maintain a safe teaching and learning environment. Some topics may trigger distress and children may be afraid of negative feedback. Therefore, reinforcing and modelling the rules along with discussion around confidentiality, mutual respect and values will help to create open and honest dialogue.

The topics covered and teaching objectives derived for each lesson have taken into account the teacher guidance: Teaching about Mental Health and Emotional Wellbeing (PSHE Association 2019) and research conducted by YoungMinds UK, a leading children's mental health charity.

The activities can be used in a variety of ways as a stimulus for discussion and thinking, such as:

- Individual children who may directly resonate with the themes
- Paired work

- Small group work

- Whole class work

- Whole school assembly

There is a growing mental health crisis in schools. Research suggests that one in ten primary school children will have a diagnosable mental health condition, rising to one in eight when we include emotional distress (YoungMinds, 2017). Preparing children for the complexities of life in an ever-changing world will help them to develop resilience and adaptability as 21st-century life-long learners.

USEFUL LINKS

Mentally Healthy Schools
Mentally Healthy Schools brings together mental health resources, advice and information for primary schools.
www.mentallyhealthyschools.org.uk

Place 2Be
Place2Be is a children's mental health charity that provides mental health support in schools through one-to-one and group counselling.
www.place2be.org.uk

Sport Inspired
Using sport-based activities, Sport Inspired works directly with children from the UK's most deprived communities who are more likely to experience mental health issues than their affluent peers.
www.sportinspired.org

Young Minds
Young Minds provides mental health support to young people, promotes good mental health and champions the voices of young people and parents to influence mental health policy and practice.
https://youngminds.org.uk

Action for Children
Action for Children protects and supports children and young people, provides practical and emotional care and support and ensures the voices of young people are heard.
www.actionforchildren.org.uk

Mind
Mind provides advice and support to empower anyone experiencing a mental health problem. They campaign to improve services, raise awareness and promote understanding.
www.mind.org.uk

The Children's Society
The Children's Society provides support to young people who face crisis; those who feel unloved, are scared or are unable to cope.
ww.childrenssociety.org.uk

Samaritans

Samaritans is dedicated to reducing feelings of isolation and disconnection that can lead to suicide.

www.samaritans.org

Education Support

Education Support is a charity dedicated to improving the health and wellbeing of teachers, teaching assistants, headteachers, lecturers and support staff in schools.

www.educationsupport.org.uk

Mental Health Foundation

The Mental Health Foundation is a UK charity, whose mission is to help people to thrive through understanding, protecting and sustaining their mental health.

www.mentalhealth.org.uk

Kids Health

A resource for parents, teachers and children. It provides lesson plans and information on health and wellbeing.

https://kidshealth.org

The Kaleidoscope Plus Group

A leading national mental health and wellbeing charity that champions change, promotes positive mental health and wellbeing and delivers valuable services to communities.

www.kaleidoscopeplus.org.uk

Sporting Equals

Sporting Equals is a charity that champions work on equality and inclusion through campaigning and research.

www.sportingequals.org.uk

Show Racism the Red Card

Show Racism the Red Card is an anti-racism charity that champions equality, diversity and inclusion using the power of football. They work with schools across the UK.

www.theredcard.org

Inside Inclusion

Inside Inclusion develops network groups and establishes diversity and inclusion committees to drive internal change. They also help to incorporate inclusion into strategic planning.

https://insideinclusion.com

Just Like Us
Just Like Us is an LGBTQ+ charity for young people. It partners with employers to train LGBTQ+ young people to give talks, workshops and use their own stories to champion equality and challenge prejudice.
www.justlikeus.org

Believe Perform
Believe Perform provides content on performance psychology, wellbeing and mental health content for the sporting community.
www.believeperform.com

PART I

FEELINGS AND EMOTIONS

The resources in this section provide children with an opportunity to explore the definition of mental health and ways in which they can keep a healthy mind, introducing them to mindfulness and strategies to keep calm. They will also have the opportunity to think about how emotions and mood can change depending on the circumstance, and ways in which they can manage big and negative feelings.

Activity 1

WHAT IS MENTAL HEALTH?

Age: 7–11

Context

Our mental health is part of the way in which we live our lives every day. Generating open and collaborative discussions around what this looks like, and more specifically what this means to different children, is vital to ensuring that they feel safe to talk about their feelings and emotions.

Learning outcomes

The children will have an opportunity to:

- Understand the definition of mental health

- Recognise and respond to a wider range of feelings

- Understand good and not so good feelings and associated language

- Recognise that they may experience conflicting emotions

- Reflect on what positively and negatively affects their mental health

Activity

This activity provides children with an opportunity to explore the definition of mental health and what this looks like for them. Pose the question: What does mental health mean to you? Encourage children to explore different things that make up our mental health. This could include feelings, managing change, exercise or resilience. Due to the stigma associated with mental health, ensure that the children are aware that mental health is not always negative, rather it is a part of how we feel which in turn affects how we live our lives everyday.

The mental health jigsaw can be used to generate discussion around feelings that make up our mental health. Ask the children to consider what can cause someone to express the feelings that they can see on the resource.

Use the blank mental health jigsaw resource to provide children with an opportunity to draw the things that they feel make up their mental health based on earlier discussions, and support their drawings with a caption.

Questions for thinking

- What do you understand by mental health?
- What does mental health mean to you?
- How do you think the characters in the resource are feeling?
- What might have happened to make the characters feel that way?
- Can you think of a time when you have experienced any of these feelings?

Resources

- Mental health jigsaw
- Mental health jigsaw (blank)

Mental health jigsaw

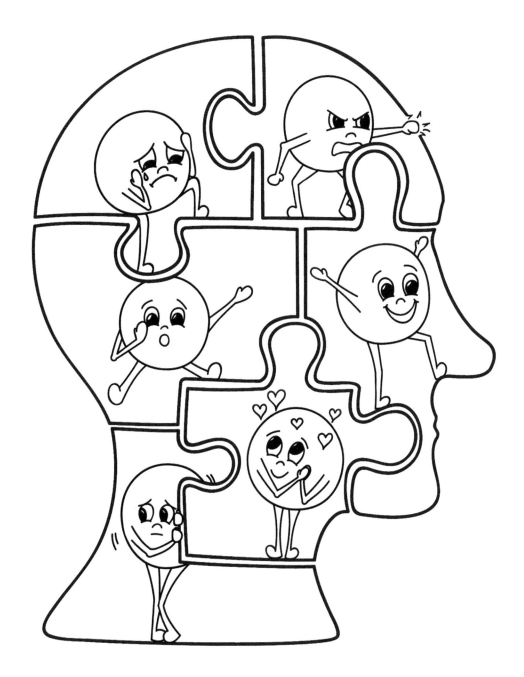

Mental health jigsaw (blank)

Activity 2

MY MINDFUL MIND

Age: 7–11

Context

Mindfulness is a technique that you can learn which involves making an effort to notice what is happening in the present moment in your mind, body and surroundings. Mindfulness can help children become more self-aware, feel calmer and be able to cope with difficult thoughts. Mindfulness can be used when children feel anxiety, nervousness or fear. Like positive mental health, it can enable children to feel happy, safe and well by being able to make choices on how they respond to their thoughts and feelings.

Learning outcomes

The children will have an opportunity to:

- Think about how to keep a mindful mind

- Recognise and respond to a wider range of feelings

- Understand good and not so good feelings and associated language

- Recognise that they may experience conflicting emotions

- Reflect on what positively and negatively affects their mental health

Activity

This activity provides children with an opportunity to develop social and emotional skills by identifying feelings, thoughts and emotions. Pose the question: What does having a healthy mind mean to you? Encourage children to provide a reason and lead this onto a discussion on wellness and being mindful. Pose the question: What do you do when things get really busy and you find yourself having to multi-task? Explain to the children that different situations can cause their mind to get very busy and sometimes it can become overwhelming – this can cause worry and anxiety.

Tell the children that they are going to think of things that they can do to help them keep a mindful mind. A mindful mind can help them to keep focus, pay attention and notice what is happening around them and how it is making them feel. Let them know that being mindful can help them to cope and manage with big emotions and challenging experiences, just like a muscle. It's something that they can build with practice.

Questions for thinking

- What does having a healthy mind mean to you?
- What do you do to manage big feelings?
- What can you do to be mindful?
- How will you use your mindful strategies?
- When will you practice your mindful strategies?

Resources

- My mindful mind

My mindful mind

Activity 3

SMALL AND BIG FEELINGS

Age: 7–11

Context

We will experience a range of feelings and emotions through our lives and our mood can be affected by different situations and circumstance. It is important that children understand how their emotional state can affect the way that they think and behave in addition to the impact of the expression of their feelings on others. Children should know that their emotions are valid and that finding socially acceptable ways of how they express these emotions will help them to cope with big feelings.

Learning outcomes

The children will have an opportunity to:

- Recognise and respond to a wider range of feelings

- Understand good and not so good feelings and associated language

- Recognise that they may experience conflicting emotions

- Reflect upon how they would react in different situations

Activity

This activity provides children with an opportunity to explore emotional state through a range of scenarios. Explain to the children that they are going to be talking about feelings. Pose the question: What do feelings mean to you? What are small and big feelings?

Children may begin by experiencing small feelings, which can spiral and manifest into big feelings. However, this will be determined by the individual as well as external factors. A word wall on the board could be generated with small and big feelings.

Use the associated feeling cards to stimulate discussion on small and big feelings, guided by the questions for thinking. Encourage children to think about their response mechanism to, during and after the example that they have provided and possible impact on others.

Questions for thinking

- Can you think of an example of when you have felt this way and why?

- Did your reaction affect others? If so, how?

- How would you help someone to manage sad feelings?

- What are the benefits of managing sad feelings?

- How do you manage big feelings?

Resources

- Feeling words

Feeling words

Angry	Hopeful	Sad
Happy	Excited	Worried
Stressed	Annoyed	Compassionate
Bored	Jealous	Tired
Surprised	Kind	Scared
Confident	Disappointed	Ashamed
Depressed	Nervous	Loved
Lonely	Proud	Embarrassed

Activity 4

HOW WOULD YOU FEEL?

Age: 7–11

Context

No matter how children feel – good or bad – it is healthy to help them to put their feelings into words. Talking about feelings will help them to feel close to people who care and help towards building trust and openness so that they feel comfortable to express how they feel in any given situation. This activity will help children to put feelings into words and think about strategies that they can use to help with emotional control.

Learning outcomes

The children will have an opportunity to:

- Recognise and respond to a wider range of feelings

- Understand good and not so good feelings and associated language

- Recognise that they may experience conflicting emotions

- Reflect upon how they would react in different situations

- Identify strategies for emotional regulation

Activity

Use the associated feeling cards to stimulate discussion about mood and feelings as a lesson starter. Pose children a variety of questions when using the associated feeling words: How are you feeling today? Who felt anxious about leading the class assembly? Who is excited about the school trip tomorrow?

The scenario cards can be used to guide discussion about response, empathy and strategies for managing feelings. Ask the children to work in groups to talk about each scenario and encourage them to:

- Provide a response to each scenario
- Consider the impact negative feelings can have on behaviours
- Reflect on the impact negative behaviours can have on others and relationships
- Provide a strategy for managing negative feelings

Emotional regulation encompasses both positive and negative feelings. Helping children to notice what they are feeling and naming it is a great step towards emotional regulation.

Questions for thinking

- How do you feel after reading each scenario?
- Can you explain why you feel this way?
- Put yourself in the shoes of the characters; how would you respond and why?
- What advice would you give to help them manage their feelings?

Resources

- Feeling words
- Feeling scenario cards

Feeling words

Angry	Hopeful	Sad
Happy	Excited	Worried
Stressed	Annoyed	Compassionate
Bored	Jealous	Tired
Surprised	Kind	Scared
Confident	Disappointed	Ashamed
Depressed	Nervous	Loved
Lonely	Proud	Embarrassed

Feeling scenario cards

You have just found out that you have not been selected to take part in the National Chess Championship for your school team.	You are the goalkeeper for your school team. There are only 5 minutes left to play. You miss a penalty save and your team lose.	Roopjot supports Chelsea Ladies and has just found out that the players and the manager are going to visit her school to lead on an assembly.
Nimesh invited his best friend Gemma to a training session at his local rugby club. His friends giggled when they saw Gemma.	Both you and your best friend enter a prize draw to watch a match in an executive box at Wembley Stadium. You find out that your best friend has won the prize.	You have not completed your homework task. As a result, you are not allowed to play with your friends during lunch-time play.
You find out that your classmate has been saying nasty things about you to others. Everyone at school is now starting and laughing at you.	Yasmin loves football and joined the after-school football club. When she arrived she found out that she was the only girl to join.	You have been asked by your PE teacher to speak at a tournament. There are over 100 parents and friends watching in the crowd.
Zeena beat her opponent using a double step-over and was able to drive away with speed to take a shot at goal and score.	The referee has asked you to re-take a free-kick that you previously scored. This time you miss. You shout at the referee who then asks you to leave the pitch. Your team now have to play with one	It is the start of the new year. You are in the changing rooms and all your teammates are showing each other their new trainers. You have your old trainers from last year.

Activity 5

EMOTIONAL ROLLERCOASTER

Age: 7–11

Context

Children will experience lots of highs and lows and at times in rapid succession. They will go through situations that make them feel excited, exhilarated and happy, to sad, disappointed and frustrated. This rollercoaster of emotions can cause emotional suffering leading to poor self-care, personality change and withdrawal. It is therefore important that children are given the opportunity to reflect upon the ways in which they can control, regulate and self-manage their emotions and recognise their impact on others.

Learning outcomes

The children will have an opportunity to:

- Reflect upon feelings and emotions expressed in a day

- Recognise how feelings change over time

- Understand that people are affected by different things and in different ways

- Discuss factors that influence their personal choices

Activity

This activity allows children to discuss the factors that influence their mood, behaviours and personal decisions. Tell the children that they are going to be thinking about the feelings that they may go through at different points of the day. Provide children with the emotional rollercoaster graph which they will use to plot points that illustrate their emotions.

Read out the 10 sentences from the "Rollercoaster scenarios" resource and ask the children to plot points to best identify where these feelings would be on the graph. They can also name the feeling word next to each point. Once they have plotted all the points, ask them to join the dots to create their rollercoaster. They can share their rollercoaster with a friend and compare similarities and differences.

Questions for thinking

- How does the situation that we are in affect our mood and emotions?

- At what point did you feel happy? Why?

- In what situation did you feel nervous or anxious?

- Can you name the feeling words that you have noted on your rollercoaster? How did these change over the course of the day?

- How can we manage our mood in some of these situations? Who can support you?

Resources

- Rollercoaster scenarios

- Emotional rollercoaster graph

Rollercoaster scenarios

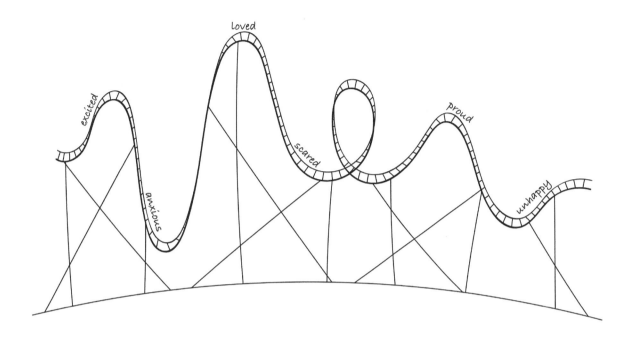

You wake up to an early birthday present.

You are running late for school and accidentally spill cereal over your school uniform.

Your teacher tells you that you are going to sit a maths test.

Your best friend shares their favourite break time treat with you.

You score a goal for your class football team.

You fall over in the playground and think that someone pushed you over on purpose.

The head-teacher asks you to deliver the school assembly in front of 100 children.

You feel someone tap you on the shoulder. When you turn around, there is nobody there.

You have PE in the afternoon but have forgotten your PE kit.

You receive the spelling test award at school.

Emotional rollercoaster graph

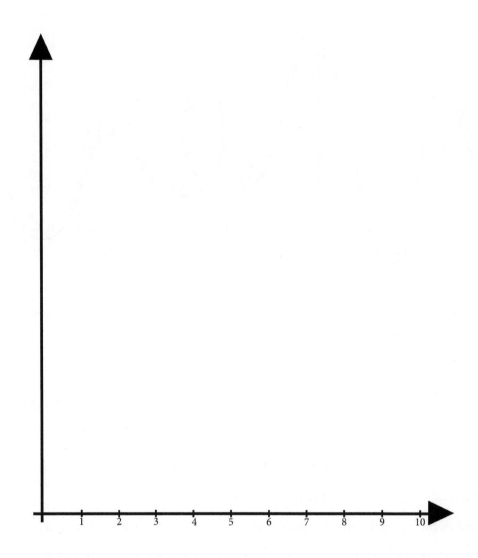

Activity 6

KEEPING CALM

Age 7–11

Context

Children who understand their emotions and those who are able to find ways of managing distress and negative feelings will be in a better position to have the resilience to manage difference and adversity throughout their lives. Being calm helps children to have more control over their emotions, encourages them to notice their responses, be grateful, hear their own thoughts and enjoy better health.

Learning outcomes

The children will have an opportunity to:

- Understand good and not so good feelings and associated language

- Identify situations that have caused a range of feelings

- Explore similarities and differences in these feelings with that of others

- Understand that everyone will have a different response mechanism

- Reflect on how your response and behaviours impact on others

Activity

This activity will allow children to identify situations that have led to them to feel in a particular way and how they can manage their responses to any negative feelings, which will help them to maintain calmness and a healthy mind.

Use the feeling cards with a focus on negative feelings. Choose a word and use this as an example to demonstrate when you felt this way. For example: Anxious – "I remember feeling really anxious on the day of my driving test. I had already failed twice and was scared I might fail again." Ask the children if they have ever felt nervous or frustrated before and in what situation.

Tell the children that people who study the brain have found that movement and exercise can help with managing stress and big emotions. Ask the children to discuss the exercises that they could use to help them manage how they feel so that they can keep calm. Invite them to create a poster illustrating exercises or techniques that can be used as calming down techniques. Some examples are visualising a quiet place, jumping, stretching, drinking water etc. They can also try these in action too.

Questions for thinking

- What can trigger your response mechanisms to situations in your life?
- How can you manage negative emotions?
- How can you use movement and exercise to help you manage big feelings?
- How do your responses affect others?

Resources

- Feeling words
- Keeping calm poster

Feeling words

Angry	Hopeful	Sad
Happy	Excited	Worried
Stressed	Annoyed	Compassionate
Bored	Jealous	Tired
Surprised	Kind	Scared
Confident	Disappointed	Ashamed
Depressed	Nervous	Loved
Lonely	Proud	Embarrassed

Keeping calm

PART II

BULLYING

The resources in this section provide children with an opportunity to recognise the impact of bullying, including keeping safe online. They will also be able to explore and discuss strategies that they can use if they or a friend is victim to bullying.

Activity 7

RAJ AND HIS LOVE FOR FOOTBALL

Age: 7–11

Context

Bullying can take different forms such as emotional, verbal, physical or sexual. Bullying is usually understood as behaviour by an individual or group, repeated over time, that is intended to hurt others. It is important that children understand asking for help and talking to someone about the challenges that they might be facing will have a positive impact on their mental health and overall wellbeing.

Learning outcomes

The children will have an opportunity to:

- Recognise and respond to a wider range of feelings

- Understand the definition of bullying

- Recognise feelings associated with bullying

- Understand the impact of bullying on our mental health

- Recognise when and how to ask for help

Activity

Introduce the lesson by asking children to generate their own definition of bullying. Pose the question: What does bullying mean to you? What words would you associate with bullying?

A definition that could be used to introduce children to the concept of bullying is: "Treating others unfairly due to individual difference." This could be related to all protected characteristics under the Equality Act (2010).

Use the "Raj and his love for football" story to provide children with an opportunity to engage in discussion around the concept of bullying using Raj as the character. The questions for thinking can be used to help children infer and develop:

- Empathy for how Raj is feeling
- Reasoning skills when considering the information in the story
- Justification and rationale for what they think and why

It is important that the children can illustrate empathy and compassion for how Raj is feeling and begin to consider strategies for support.

Questions for thinking

- Can you identify how Raj is feeling?
- How would you feel if that was you?
- What do you think Raj should do?
- What would you do in this situation and why?

Resources

- Raj and his love for football

Raj and his love for football

Raj has missed the last 3 training sessions for his school football team.

"Coach Sophie, I have a dentist appointment after school today."

"Coach Sophie, my ankle is really sore!"

"I am really sorry – my mum has asked me to help her with a few things after school today."

His coach is worried about him, but every time she has asked, "Raj, is everything ok?" he would reply, "Yes Coach Sophie, I love playing football for the school team and will be at training next week."

He is tired of being the last out of the changing rooms, because his teammates have hidden his football socks.

He is tired of having to walk home hungry after training, because his teammates have taken his pocket money.

He is tired of being laughed at, every time he dribbles and loses the ball.

He is tired of his teammates being mean to him.

Raj is slowly losing his love for playing for the school football team.

Activity 8

HELPING RAJ

Age: 8–11

Context

Almost everyone will be affected by bullying during their life. This can be as a child or as a young person or it can happen as an adult in work; it can even be as an elderly person in the community. Children should know and understand that bullying in any form aims to hurt an individual or a group. Bullying happens more than once and can impact upon self-esteem and confidence.

Learning outcomes

The children will have an opportunity to:

- Recognise and respond to a wider range of feelings

- Understand the definition of bullying

- Recognise feelings associated with bullying

- Understand the impact of bullying on our mental health

- Recognise when and how to ask for help

Activity

This lesson can be used as a follow-up from Activity 7. Ask the children to reflect upon the story about Raj who was being bullied at his football club. Pose the question: What do you remember when we read the story about Raj? How were you left feeling after you heard that he was being treated unfairly?

The Helping Raj resource can help children to consider support mechanisms that could help Raj to find a solution and in turn, re-ignite his love for football. The discussion can also be made relevant to your school, considering what the children would do if they themselves or a friend is victim to bullying.

It is important that children are able to recognise who they can turn to for support and feel safe to do so when they are facing challenges.

As an extension, the children could write an informal letter of advice to Raj and think about how this letter will support Raj to manage how he is feeling.

Questions for thinking

- What advice would you give to Raj and how do you think this will help him?
- Why is seeking help important?
- Who can you seek support from at school?
- How would you help Raj so that he feels confident to return to training?

Resources

- Helping hands

Helping hands

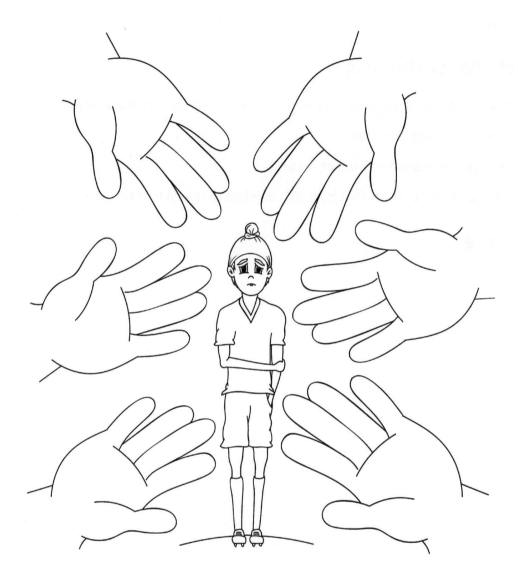

Activity 9

IS THIS A STRANGER DANGER TYPE OF THING?

Age: 9–11

Context

Online abuse is any type of abuse that happens on the internet facilitated through technology like phones, computers, games or tablets. Technology can give perpetrators of abuse easier access to children and can include cyberbullying, emotional abuse, sexting, sexual abuse or sexual exploitation. Children can also be groomed online where perpetrators may use online platforms to build trusting relationships. Online abuse can lead to anxiety, suicidal thoughts, self-harm or eating disorders (HM Government, 2017).

Learning outcomes

The children will have an opportunity to:

- Understand the definition of online abuse

- Recognise how online abuse can occur

- Recognise and identify how to keep safe online

- Identify ways in which they can seek support

Activity

This lesson should be delivered as an integrated part of keeping safe online and work on online abuse should be done prior to delivering this activity. Cyberbullying can cause children to feel frightened and helpless and can have a detrimental impact on their emotional health. Research suggests that online abuse can lead to nightmares, poor attendance, behavioural changes, social withdrawal, low self-esteem or depression.

The lesson could begin with a reflection exercise based on what the children already know and understand about cyberbullying. Pose the questions: What online forms of technology do you currently use and why? What do understand about cyberbullying? What do you do to keep safe when using these online platforms?

The poem on cyberbullying can be used to promote discussion around the psychological impact of cyberbullying, how to keep safe online and how to respond if there is a cause for concern.

Questions for thinking

- What does cyberbully mean?
- What is online abuse?
- Why is it important to keep safe online?
- How can you keep safe online?
- What advice would you give to the child?

Resources

Poem – Is this a stranger danger type of thing?

Is this a stranger danger type of thing?

Last night I got a message.
I would say, just after nine.
It popped up in the corner
of a game I play online.

I was tapping on my keyboard,
just the way I always do,
when there it was in front of me.
"Hello, from me to you."

The user name was "Hunter Dude,"
which sounded like a guy.
But, though I didn't know him,
I decided to reply.

I asked him what was happening?
He wrote, "Just chillin' out."
I said, "This game is awesome."
And he messaged me, "No doubt."

We spoke of our adventures
in the many different worlds.
"Are you a boy?" he asked me.
And I wrote, "No, I'm a girl."

He didn't answer right away.
I had to wait a while.
Then he sent me an emoji,
with a cheesy looking smile.

I asked him why he messaged me?
He said he liked my name.
I'm Jumping Jay-Jay Mercury,
at least while playing games.

We talked about a lot of things,
like movies, pets, and school,
and all the bands we listened to.
He sounded pretty cool.

I asked the guy how old he was,
as it was hard to tell.
He sent me back a silly joke.
I answered, "LOL."

"So, where'd you live?" he said to me.
"Perhaps you'd like to meet?
I know we're bound to get along,
cos you sound really sweet."

I must admit, I blushed a bit,
and didn't know what to say.
Should I write back and answer, "Yes!"
or tell him, "Go away!"

But in the end, I said, "It's late.
I've got to go, my friend.
I'll be on here tomorrow night,
Let's talk about it then."

I thought about it in my dreams,
and all throughout the day.
Was this a stranger danger thing,
or would it be okay?

So, now I'm sitting here again,
deciding what to do.
Should I meet up with Hunter Dude?
I'm tempted, but would you?

Activity 10

CYBERBULLYING

Age: 9–11

Context

Online abuse can affect children at home as well as at school. Through the virtual world, it can be difficult to identify who the bully is and over the internet, the reach is vast and some children may not even realise that they are being bullied.

Learning outcomes

The children will have an opportunity to:

- Understand the definition of online abuse

- Recognise how online abuse can occur

- Recognise and identify how to keep safe online

- Identify ways in which they can seek support

Activity

This lesson can be used as a follow-up to Activity 9. Ask the children to reflect upon the definition of online abuse and what this looks like, using the poem as a reference. Pose the question: What does cyberbullying look like? Talk through responses in detail, providing them with an opportunity to respond and challenge. You might use the following statements to provoke thinking:

- Simran has received several abusive messages through an online game

- Darnell arrived at school only to find out that someone has been texting embarrassing photos of him

- Toby has been receiving threatening text messages and is being bullied into giving away his brand new bike

Ask the children to consider what they would do and the advice that they would provide Simran, Darnell and Toby. In this lesson, the children can work independently or as a group to create a poster that highlights top tips for keeping safe online using a template. You might consider the following: Keep passwords a secret; Never give out personal information; Avoid responding to messages from people you do not know.

Questions for thinking

- What does cyberbully mean?
- What does online abuse look like?
- What is the impact of online abuse?
- How can you keep safe online?

Resources

- Keeping safe online – Top tips

Keeping safe online – Top tips!

PART III

GROWTH AND FIXED MINDSET

The resources in this section provide children with an opportunity to reflect upon the difference between a growth and fixed mindset and strategies that they can use to help them cultivate a growth mindset through goal setting and practising gratitude.

Activity 11

GROWTH AND FIXED MINDSET

Age: 7–11

Context

A growth mindset can promote greater learning and fosters resilience and a love for learning. Creating a growth mindset environment can aid children to view challenges as a tool for self-growth by being persistent and finding different ways of solving problems. Through practice and experience, children can build knowledge and acquire skills; however, the environment that you create will help them to cultivate these skills and apply them to their everyday lives.

Learning outcomes

The children will have an opportunity to:

- Understand the definition of a growth mindset

- Recognise how to develop a growth mindset

- Recognise the differences between a growth and fixed mindset

Activity

Explain that the terms growth and fixed mindsets describe how we face challenges and setbacks. Write on the board: People with a growth mindset believe that their abilities can improve with effort and practice. People with a fixed mindset think that their abilities cannot change, no matter how hard they try.

The growth and fixed mindset statements can provide children with an opportunity to work collaboratively, develop reasoning skills and justify their thinking whilst placing the statements under the appropriate headings. They can also think about how these statements relate to them as learners.

Questions for thinking

- What can you do if you find something difficult?
- What tools can help you to learn and get better at something?
- What is a growth mindset learner?
- What is a fixed mindset learner?

Resources

- Growth and fixed mindset statements
- Growth and fixed mindset

Growth and fixed mindset statements

Will not give up.	Will give up easily.
Is open to learning.	Is closed to learning.
Is willing to try new things, even if it is challenging.	Has a fear of failure and will not try new things.
Learns by asking questions.	Thinks that asking questions will not help learning.
Learns from feedback and uses this to help learning.	Ignores feedback and thinks that it will not help learning.
Takes responsibility to learn from setbacks.	Will blame others for setbacks.
Is inspired by other people.	Is threatened by other people.
Finds different ways to learn.	Will use the same method to learn.
Believes that effort and practice can help them to learn.	Believes that their abilities cannot change, not matter how hard they try.

Growth and fixed mindset

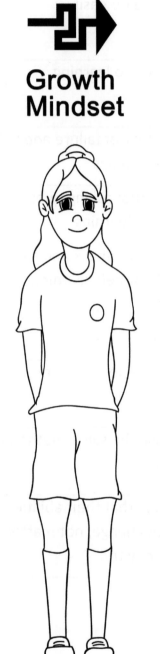

Growth Mindset

Fixed Mindset

Activity 12

SUPER STRENGTHS

Age: 7–11

Context

Cultivating an environment that helps children to develop a growth mindset will give them a sense of purpose and make them value the process over the end result. The use of language is important, so replacing the word "failing" with the word "learning" can change the way in which children respond to challenges. In building a growth mindset you can help to develop resilience, moulding the mind so that children are open to taking the opportunities that are presented to them with openness, grit and desire.

Learning outcomes

The children will have an opportunity to:

- Reflect upon the definition of a growth mindset

- Recognise how to develop a growth mindset

- Recognise the differences between a growth and fixed mindset

Activity

This lesson can be used as a follow-up to Activity 11. Ask the children to reflect upon the definition of a growth and fixed mindset. Pose the question: What does mindset mean to you? What do you now understand about a growth mindset? What about a fixed mindset? How are they different?

This lesson will focus on strength-based learning, looking at what the individual can do as opposed to what they can't. Ask the children to work in pairs to consider their strengths. Then, pose the question: If you want to turn these strengths into super strengths, what do you need to do?

Encourage the children to consider the growth mindset steps that they will take in cultivating their superpower. The children can use the Superhero resource to record their strengths and the actions that they will take to enhance these, turning them into super strengths.

Questions for thinking

- What is a growth and fixed mindset learner?

- How do you know this?

- Can you identify your strength?

- What evidence suggests that this is a strength?

- What tools will you use to turn this into a super strength?

Resources

- Superhero

Superhero

Activity 13

GOAL SETTING

Age: 7–11

Context

Goal setting will help children to think critically about their intentions in life. Goals help children to visualise what they want to achieve and the steps that they need to take in order to help them. Goal setting gives children something to strive for and teaches them to take responsibility for their own behaviours and learning. It can help them to develop a growth mindset and build a powerful lifelong habit.

Learning outcomes

The children will have an opportunity to:

- Recognise the importance of goal setting

- Recognise how to set specific and measurable goals

- Identify strategies that will help towards achieving goals

- Identify ways in which children can take responsibility for goal setting

Activity

This activity provides children with an opportunity to explore goal-setting techniques and recognise how setting goals can help them to be better learners. Begin by looking for ways that the children already use goal-setting techniques. Pose the question: Can you think of something that you had always longed for and worked hard to get? Explore how these accomplishments made the children feel and breakdown the techniques that they used to help them.

Ask the children to think about the difference between small and big goals and if techniques in trying to achieve them differ. Discuss how different techniques can be used to meet a range of challenges and that this might look different for each person. A small goal can be described as something that can be achieved in a short space of time whereas a big goal might take a little longer.

The children can use the "My goals" resource to set their big and small goals and consider the techniques that will help towards achieving them.

Questions for thinking

- What does goal setting mean to you?
- What are big goals?
- What are small goals?
- What techniques can you use to help you achieve your goals?

Resources

- My goals

My goals

MY BIG GOAL

HOW WILL I ACHIEVE IT?

MY SMALL GOAL

MY SMALL GOAL

HOW WILL I ACHIEVE IT?

HOW WILL I ACHIEVE IT?

Activity 14

LET'S CELEBRATE

Age: 7–11

Context

Children should have the opportunity to share and recognise their achievements and most importantly celebrate the things that are most important to them. Enabling them to feel good about themselves will have a positive impact on their mental health and wellbeing. The power of praise and acknowledging effort can be an effective way of boosting self-esteem and motivation in children.

Learning outcomes

The children will have an opportunity to:

- Recognise and respond to a wider range of feelings

- Discuss what positively and negatively affects our mental health

- Reflect on and celebrate achievements

- Recognise the impact of acknowledging achievements on our mental health

Activity

Tell the children that they are going to be reflecting on things that have made them feel good and better about themselves. No matter how big or small, their accomplishments are important which is why you want them to be shared. Start by giving the children your personal example. Make it as light-hearted and fun as possible to allow the children to recognise that accomplishments can take a range of forms and personal to the individual.

The "Let's celebrate" cards can be used to generate discussion and associated feelings.

The children can then jot down an achievement that they are most proud of, but to keep this anonymous. Gather these together and sit the children in a horseshoe shape, ready to share in the form of a "Guess Who?" During the celebration and sharing, encourage the children to provide a reason for their noted achievement.

Questions for thinking

- How would you feel in each of those situations?

- Do any of those achievements resonate with you?

- How does celebrating achievements help maintain good mental health?

Resources

- Let's celebrate cards

Let's celebrate cards

"I have been practicing so much and have finally faced my fear of climbing up a wall close to 40 metres in height. I just can't believe it!	"With my dad's help, I was able to make my lunch for school".	"I woke up early to walk to school with my mum, rather than drive in as we usually do".
"I find it really difficult to read. I don't actually like reading that much. But today I read the 1st page of my school book to my sister".	"In PE, I was able to balance on one leg for 3 seconds! My teacher Mr Hall was very impressed".	"A new player came to train with us at our athletics club. I helped her make friends – she had the best session!"
"I did much better in my spelling test."	"Me and my best friend Andrew stayed in during lunchtime to help our hockey coach tidy and organise the equipment in our sports cupboard".	"With the help of my sister I am now able to hula-hoop!"
"I used a double step-over to beat Carly in football. I can't wait to try more skills when we train again".	"I had the courage to stand-up on stage during our class assembly".	"I gave a homeless person my sandwich and bottle of water".

Activity 15

TREE OF GROWTH

Age: 7–11

Context

It is important to help children understand that every achievement is valued, no matter how small. Celebrating accomplishments is a way of building self-confidence and driving motivation because it reinforces the meaning behind hard work and dedication. Increased levels of self-esteem can help children towards achieving their next goal.

Learning outcomes

The children will have an opportunity to:

- Recognise and respond to a wider range of feelings

- Discuss what positively and negatively affects our mental health

- Understand the importance of celebrating achievements

- Recognise the impact of acknowledging achievements on our mental health

Activity

Invite the children to reflect upon the definition of achievements and why they should be celebrated. Pose the questions: What does achievement mean to you? Why do you think we should celebrate achievements? A list can be formulated on the benefits of recognising achievements. The following can be used as a guide:

- Boost self-esteem and motivation

- Developing a growth and success mindset

- Taking inspiration and learning to adapt to enhance learning

- Happy chemicals – release of dopamine which makes us feel good

- Sharing success and learning from each other

Explain to the children that achievements occur in small steps and with a great deal of hard work and effort – everyone is capable of achieving something. Ask them to recall their most memorable achievements and justify a reason why they were such an achievement.

The children can use the "Tree of growth" to write down or draw their achievements and why they are most proud of them.

Questions for thinking

- What does achievement mean to you?

- What tools and skills help you to achieve?

- What are the benefits of celebrating achievements?

- Can you identify your most memorable achievements?

- Can you provide a reason why you are most proud of them?

Resources

- Tree of growth

Tree of growth

Activity 16

GRATITUDE

Age: 7–11

Context

Helping children to cultivate an attitude of gratitude can increase happiness, help them to have a positive view of life and teach them to be more empathetic. Gratitude teaches children to be thankful for everything that they have, no matter what this might be. Expressing gratitude will aid children in feeling positive emotions and embracing good experiences, improve their health, help them to deal with adversity and to build strong relationships, leading to positive mental health.

Learning outcomes

The children will have an opportunity to:

- Recognise the definition of gratitude
- Identify how children can show gratitude
- Recognise the benefits of showing gratitude on emotional health

Activity

This activity provides children with an opportunity to reflect and think about the importance of gratitude and the impact being thankful can have on their mental health. Pose the question: What does gratitude mean to you? Ask the children to discuss the things that they are thankful for and justify why. Explain that gratitude is a thankful appreciation for something that someone receives and with gratitude, they can acknowledge the goodness in their lives.

Tell the children to discuss what they think are the benefits of demonstrating and expressing gratitude. You can use the following to facilitate discussion:

- Enhances relationships and friendships
- Helps you feel better about yourself

- Reduces negative emotions
- Enhances empathy

Ask the children to write down the things that they are grateful for using the Showing gratitude resource, reflecting upon the discussions. The children should recognise the positive impact being grateful can have on their emotional health.

Questions for thinking

- What does gratitude mean to you?
- How do you express gratitude?
- What are you grateful for?
- What are the benefits of expressing gratitude?

Resources

- Showing gratitude

Showing gratitude

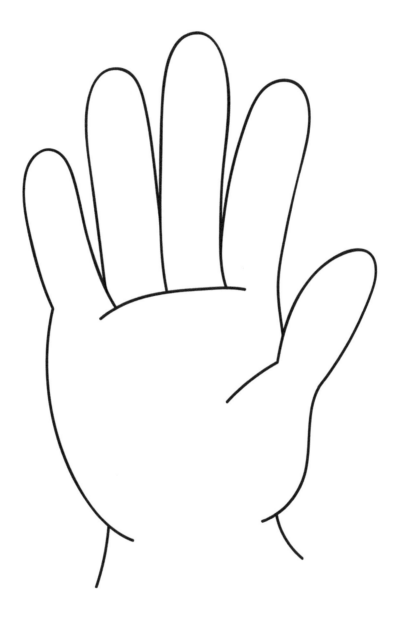

Activity 17

IMPLEMENTING CHANGE

Age: 8–11

Context

Children are changemakers. Through working collaboratively, they have the power to influence change and create a world that promotes fairness and social inclusion. As lifelong learners, children are learning to become more adaptable to the 21st-century world and resilient to the adversities that they may face throughout life. Empowering children to be advocates for mental health will help to eradicate stigma that exists around the subject.

Learning outcomes

The children will have an opportunity to:

- Understand their rights and responsibilities as young people
- Recognise how they can create and influence change
- Recognise the importance of being a change maker
- Recognise the role of voluntary and community groups
- Identify ways in which they can support mental health in their environment

Activity

Tell the children that they are going to work together to help find solutions that can help to promote mental health in their school. As changemakers, they have the power to create change and make the world a better place through open dialogue around mental health. Pose the question: What would you change and why?

Ask the children to generate a list of things that they could do to champion mental health and diversity in their school. This could also include things that they want to implement as individuals e.g. gratitude journals, friendship buddies, mindfulness exercises etc.

Using the "Action plan" resource, the children have to write an action plan that captures one of the ideas generated to then put into action within their school. They should focus on a specific thing that they would like to action and the steps that they will take in order for this to be achieved.

Questions for thinking

- What is a changemaker?

- Why is the role of a changemaker important?

- Why is talking openly about mental health important?

- What can you do to help generate open discussion around mental health?

Resources

- Action plan

Action plan

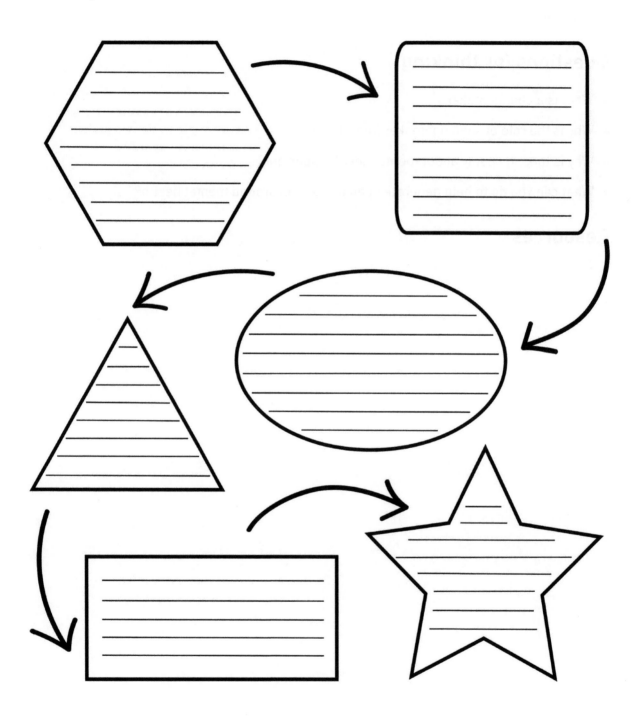

PART IV

UNDERSTANDING OURSELVES

The resources in this section provide children with an opportunity to recognise the difference between needs and wants and recognising that not everything that makes them happy costs money. They will also look at the impact of friendships on mental health and the impact of their decisions on others.

Activity 18

NEEDS AND WANTS

Age: 8–11

Context

Children live in an everchanging world influenced by what they experience, see and hear. This activity will aid understanding of the difference between what they want and what they need and how this is influenced by change in circumstance. Teaching children to differentiate between needs and wants can help develop skills for life.

Learning outcomes

The children will have an opportunity to:

- Recognise and respond to a wider range of feelings

- Recognise that they may experience conflicting emotions

- Differentiate between needs and wants

- Communicate their feelings to others

- Understand how needs and wants can change depending on circumstances

Activity

Write "Needs" and "Wants" on the whiteboard. Start by asking the children to think about what they think each word means. Provide a definition for each:

- Needs are things that we must have in order to survive.

- Wants are things that we would like to have to simply enjoy.

Use the set of Needs and Wants cards to engage children in collaborative group work, critical thinking, active listening and negotiating skills. They are required to separate the cards into two categories. They may also consider adding their own examples, providing a reason for their choice. Ask children to consider how this could change determined by circumstance.

Allow children to further develop discussion in relation to those who may not be in a position to have their needs met sufficiently and the impact this can potentially have on their health and wellbeing.

Questions for thinking

- What if the heating in your home had stopped working during the winter, but your parents were unable to get it fixed, what would you do?

- What if you really wanted to go on a school trip, but your parents needed to save that money to pay for the gas bill?

- How could world events change your needs and wants? Can you provide examples?

Resources

- Needs and Wants cards

Needs and Wants cards

Football boots	Cinema ticket	TV
Warmth	Football shirt	Shelter
Football match ticket	Water	Friends
Food and drink	Holiday	Love and care

Activity 19

WHAT MAKES YOU HAPPY?

Age: 8–11

Context

Children need to know that people who care about them will try their best to provide everything that they need. Helping children to understand the difference between needs and wants will set them up with good financial priorities that will benefit them later in life.

It is also important that children learn that the things that make them happy are not necessarily the things that cost money.

Learning outcomes

The children will have an opportunity to:

- Recognise and respond to a wider range of feelings
- Recognise that they may experience conflicting emotions
- Differentiate between needs and wants
- Communicate their feelings to others
- Understand how needs and wants can change depending on circumstances

Activity

This lesson can be used as a follow-up to Activity 18. Ask children to reflect upon the definition of needs and wants and most importantly, what it means to them. Pose the question: What makes you happy? Encourage the children to provide a reason. Lead this onto a discussion on cost and invite children to consider if what makes them happy also costs money.

Use the "What makes you happy?" resource and ask children to complete the Venn diagram thinking about:

- Things that make them happy

- Things that cost money

- Things that make them happy and cost money

Invite children to share, appropriately challenge, ask questions and provide justification for their thinking. Explain that although many things do cost money, there are plenty of ways in which they can be happy with things at very little or at no cost at all.

Questions for thinking

- What makes you happy?

- Do things that make you happy cost money?

- Can you think of something that does not cost money that makes you happy?

- What might cause you to feel or think that you need the latest things?

- How would you manage your emotions if there was something that you wanted, but knew that it was far too expensive?

- Should people be judged on having the latest things?

Resources

- What makes you happy?

What makes you happy?

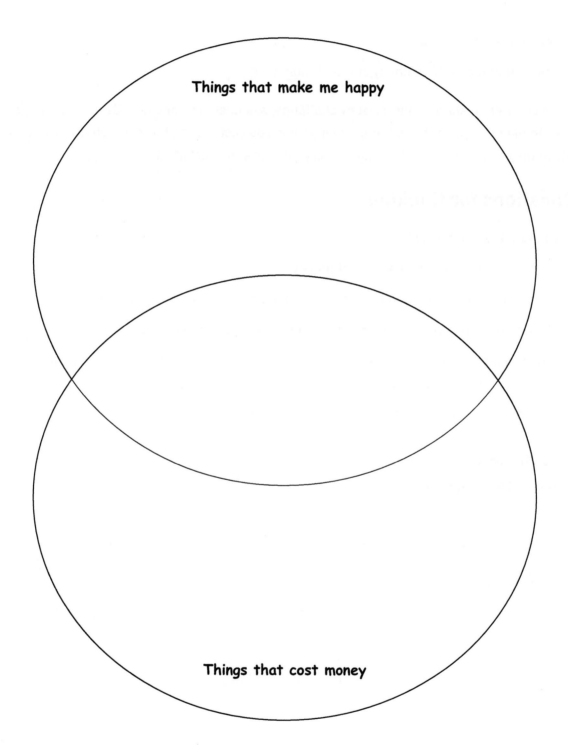

Things that make me happy

Things that cost money

Activity 20

WHAT MAKES A GOOD FRIEND?

Age: 7–11

Context

Friendships enable children to learn more about themselves and develop their own identity. For some children having the skills to make friends comes very naturally where they can share their experiences and open up to new and different people. This makes children feel good and can be a positive experience. For others, it can be challenging navigating their way to playing actively with others.

Learning outcomes

The children will have an opportunity to:

- Identify what makes a good friend

- Recognise why friendships are important

- Understand the skills needed to help make and maintain friendships

Activity

Start by asking the children to think about who they are friends with and why. Pose the question: What makes a good friend? This could be noted in the form of a concept map. Encourage children to provide a reason or evidence from their experiences of good friendships.

It is also important that children recognise that not all friendships can be a positive experience. Ask them to think about experiences of friendships that have made them feel sad and examples of what caused this sadness.

Use the "What makes a good friend?" resource to help children identify the skills needed to make and maintain active friendships. Encourage them to speak about why friendships are helpful and the positive impact friendships can have on emotional health.

Questions for thinking

- What skills and attributes make a good friend?

- How can you maintain friendships?

- Why are friendships important?

- How do friendships help with your mental health?

- What should you do if you have a negative experience with friendships?

Resources

- What makes a good friend?

What makes a good friend?

Friendships are good for Mental Health because ...

_____
_____
_____

Activity 21

MAKING FRIENDS

Age: 7–11

Context

Change can cause upset and children can experience a range of emotions and feelings as a result of moving house and attending a new school. Fear of making friends in a new environment can have a negative impact on their mental health and wellbeing. Providing opportunities in allowing children to develop empathy and associated feelings with change will help in better understanding and being able to cope in such situations.

Learning outcomes

The children will have an opportunity to:

- Recognise and respond to a wider range of feelings

- Recognise that they may experience conflicting emotions

- Discuss what positively and negatively affects our mental health

- Recognise associated feelings with change

- Learn how to communicate their feelings to others

- Identify strategies for managing change

Activity

Ask the children to reflect upon the discussions from Activity 20 on identifying what makes a good friend. Next, ask the children to think about how they would feel if their friend moved school or home meaning that they could no longer see them as often.

Following that, read the following about a young girl named Victoria.

> I want to tell you about a young girl named Victoria. She has moved house and is joining our school tomorrow. She is worried and nervous about making friends and joining her new class. In her old school she played for the school football team and was a star striker!
>
> But who will play with her now? She is anxious about not having any friends.

Introduce the role-play task, asking the children to work in small groups using the character puppets to create a short dialogue role-playing Victoria's first day at school. Ask the children to consider what they would say to Victoria, how they would respond to her feelings and how they will show empathy and support in helping her manage her first day at school.

Questions for thinking

- How would you feel if you were joining a new school for the first time?
- Can you think of a time when you have felt lonely? How did you respond to any negative emotions?
- How can you help Victoria make friends so that she does not feel so anxious and sad?
- What strategies do you think can help you to best manage in a new environment?

Resources

- Character puppets

Character puppets

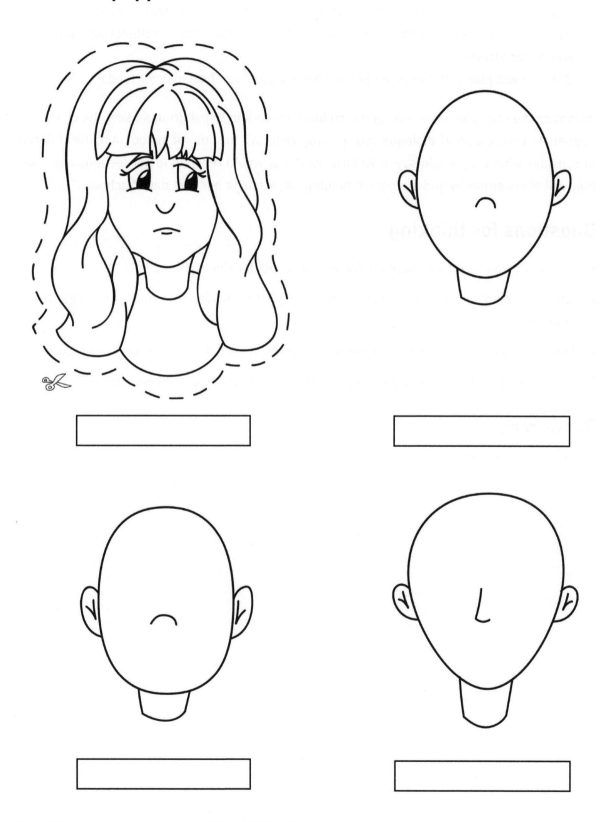

Activity 22

MANAGING DECISIONS

Age: 8–11

Context

Children make decisions all the time and as their cognitive capacity develops, they begin to rationalise and think about these decisions and the impact they have on others. Our conduct, behaviours and action can carry both positive and negative consequences. Some negative emotions may include feelings of resentment, anxiety or frustration, especially if the person feels that the decision made is unjust. This can lead to sadness and depression, having a negative impact on our mental and emotional health.

Learning outcomes

The children will have an opportunity to:

- Recognise and respond to a wider range of feelings

- Recognise that they may experience conflicting emotions

- Discuss what positively and negatively affects our mental health

- Think about the decisions that they make and the impact on others

- Recognise how to provide a rationale and justification for the decisions made

Activity

This activity provides children with an opportunity to discuss, negotiate and develop higher order thinking skills. They will be held to account for the decisions that they make and asked to provide justification and rationale. They will also need to consider how they will manage any negative emotions as a consequence of their decisions. The children will be required to work in small groups and will need a set of the "Animal cards" resource. They will then need to prepare and present their decisions at a press conference.

Read out the following which explains the task:

> Your job is to select a team of 5 that will take part in a National Football Tournament.
> You will also need to select the positions that they will play within the team.
> Additionally, you will need to choose a coach and a manager. You have a total of
> 10 animal cards; therefore, some will be left out. Make sure you are able to provide a
> reason for your selection.

Questions for thinking

- Who did you include in the team and why?

- Who did you decide would be best as the coach and manager and why?

- How will you inform the players on who is included and who did not make the selection?

- What strategies will you use to manage any negative behaviours?

Resources

- Animal cards

Animal cards

Lizard
Resourceful
Small
Camouflage
Agile

Elephant
Slow
Big   Good memory
Years of experience

Rabbit
Hops into small areas
Easily bored
Energetic   Creative

Gorilla
Team player
Assertive
Unpredictable
Dominant

Rat
Good organiser
Adaptable
Selfish
Good sense of smell

Lion
Protective
Natural leader
Lazy
Aggressive when necessary

Giraffe
Calm   Sociable
Tall – can see everything
Clumsy

Owl
Responsible
Wise
Good eyesight
Strategic

Bull
Strong   Persistent
Powerful when angry
Easily distracted

Cheetah
Can get carried away
Fast
Good listener
Determined

PART V

MANAGING LIFE AT HOME

The resources in this section provide children with an opportunity to recognise the impact of life at home on emotional health. They will look at analysing and evaluating strategies for managing difference, the role of a young carer and identify associated feelings.

Activity 23

SAMITA AND HER MUM (I)

Age: 8–11

Context

The life children experience at home will be varied and this can change at any point in their lives. Some may struggle to talk about situations of difficulty that might include financial strain perhaps caused by debt, loss of job or ill-health of a family member, which in turn can impact on their behaviour, social, physical and mental health.

Learning outcomes

The children will have an opportunity to:

- Recognise and respond to a wider range of feelings

- Recognise that they may experience conflicting emotions

- Discuss what positively and negatively affects our mental health

- Develop a sense of empathy towards others

- Share opinions on the things that matter to them

Activity

Explain to the children that you will be sharing a story about a young girl named Samita who is going through a difficult time at home. Tell the children that sometimes, things that they go through might be upsetting and it is ok to get emotional or feel sad. We want to encourage them to talk about their feelings and provide them with vital coping techniques.

Whilst listening to the story, ask the children to consider the words that they would use to describe Samita's feelings. Upon hearing the story, invite the children to share the list of words that they felt best illustrates Samita's emotional state and consider what Samita is going through and how she is responding to her circumstance.

The questions for thinking can be used to help children better understand and respond to adversities.

Questions for thinking

- How do you think Samita is feeling?

- Why is she feeling like this?

- What do you think Samita needs to make her feel happy?

- What would Samita like to have?

- How is her circumstance affecting her learning, behaviour and friendships?

- What can you do to help Samita?

Resources

- Samita's story

Samita's story

Samita is 9 years old and lives in a flat with her mum and older sister. When Samita started nursery, her mum and dad split up, leaving her mum, who was physically disabled, to take care of Samita and her sister. Her mum is unable to work.

The family receives state benefits, but this does not go very far. They cannot afford the cost of food, heating or water. Samita will often go to school without a bath or breakfast. As a result, she is often extremely tired and falls asleep in the afternoon. She has few friends and many of her classmates do not want to play with her and say that she "smells."

Samita is often unwell and has lost a considerable amount of weight due to poor nutrition. Her attendance is low which has had an effect on her reading and writing. She is disruptive in class and is constantly in trouble for not completing her homework. Most of her lunchtimes are spent in the Headteacher's office.

At home, Samita is always arguing with her mum and is upset that she cannot attend school trips, invite her friends over, join the local football club or have toys to play with. They simply do not have enough money.

Samita is teased about her shoes and clothes and some pick on her because her mum has a disability and is a wheelchair user. Samita is too ashamed and embarrassed to tell her teacher what it is like for her at home.

Every day is a struggle for Samita.

Activity 24

SAMITA AND HER MUM (II)

Age: 8–11

Context

Children may know of someone or care for a family member with a disability or have a disability themselves. With their varied experiences, this can have an impact on their emotional and mental wellbeing. It is important to openly discuss and raise awareness of what a disability may look like, acceptance and equality.

Learning outcomes

The children will have an opportunity to:

- Recognise and respond to a wider range of feelings
- Discuss what positively and negatively affects our mental health
- Learn how to communicate their feelings to others
- Reflect upon individual difference and respect for others
- Identify strategies for overcoming adversity and challenge

Activity

Using Samita's story from Activity 23 to engage children in discussion with a focus on individual difference, ask them to consider how Samita's mum finds ways of living her day-to-day life as a wheelchair user and the traits and skills that she may have to help her overcome challenging situations. Let the children know that it is ok to notice difference and ask questions; however they should recognise that showing respect, empathy and treating people with fairness, regardless of individual difference, should be part of their culture and moral responsibility.

Ask the children to create a story, using the "Storyboard" resource, based on the day in the life of Samita's mum. It is important that children understand that wheelchair users require access that will help them in doing day-to-day things – access to being able to live life everyday that perhaps people may take for granted. Encourage children to think about how people manage difference based on what they know and what they are learning.

Questions for thinking

- What does moral responsibility mean to you?

- Why do you think fairness in treatment is important?

- How can unfair treatment impact and affect the way someone feels and behaves?

- How do you think Samita's mum is able to get by day-to-day?

- Being a wheelchair user, what might she need to think about in her flat?

- What about if she wants to go to the supermarket?

- What considerations might there be for your school if you have wheelchair users?

Resources

- Storyboard – A day in the life of Samita's mum

A day in the life of Samita's mum

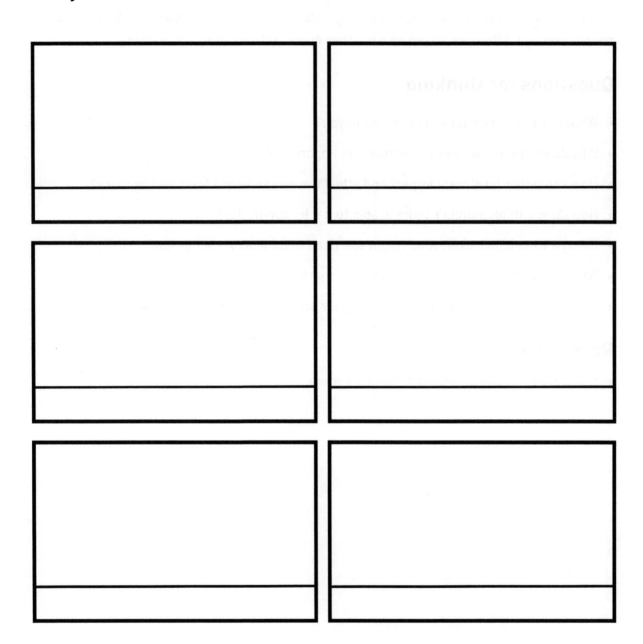

Activity 25

YOUNG CARERS (I)

Age: 8–11

Context

Young carers are forced to grow up very quickly and miss out on the same opportunities as other children because they care for family members who are disabled or chronically ill, or for adults who are misusing alcohol or drugs. You may have children in your school who are young carers and will probably experience lots of different feelings about caring. There may be times when they really enjoy helping their family, but there may be other times when they can't stand it and display frustration in just wanting to have a family like everybody else's.

Learning outcomes

The children will have an opportunity to:

- Recognise and respond to a wider range of feelings

- Discuss what positively and negatively affects our mental health

- Understand the definition of a young carer

- Explore feelings that young carers may experience

- Identify ways in which young carers can be supported

Activity

Explain to the children that they are going to be exploring something that might be sensitive and personal to them or someone that they know. If you have a young carer in your class, ensure that the learning environment to promote discussion takes sensitivity into account.

Introduce the topic of a young carer by providing context of what a young carer does. For example, a young carer is someone who takes care of a person who is unable to care for themselves. Explore and discuss what this could look like, considering physical and mental disabilities.

Young carers (I)

Use the resource "Isabella and her mum" to promote reflection and engagement around the impact of being a young carer and how they can support a young carer that they know or have in their class.

Questions for thinking

- What is a young carer?

- How are you feeling after hearing about Isabella?

- How is Isabella feeling about her situation?

- What challenges does Isabella face as a young carer?

- How would you describe Isabella as a person and why?

- What advice would you give to Isabella to help support her in her situation?

- What would you do if Isabella was your friend?

Resources

- Isabella and her mum

Isabella and her mum

Isabella is 8 years old and cares for her mum who suffers from bipolar disorder, also known as manic depression. Her mum has a fear of crowded places and has to be woken up in the morning. Her mum will only go out of the house with Isabella.

Before school, as well as getting herself dressed and ready, Isabella will wake her mum up, help her bathe and dress and make her breakfast.

When Isabella returns from school, she will help her mum make tea, go shopping and help with any household chores.

Before going to bed, she will try and finish her school homework as well as wash-up, clean and help her mum get dressed for bed.

Isabella loves her mum dearly but gets very little time to herself.

Isabella has tried to speak to her best friend about how she is feeling but doesn't think that there is any point in talking about it.

Sometimes she sits in her bedroom and cries herself to sleep.

Activity 26

YOUNG CARERS (II)

Age: 8–11

Context

Young carers take on a lot of responsibilities and it is important that children are helped to better understand the role of a young carer in order to be able to empathise and provide support. It is also important that teachers are aware of any young carers that they may have in their school so that they can plan for and put in place appropriate intervention and provision.

Learning outcomes

The children will have an opportunity to:

- Recognise and respond to a wider range of feelings

- Discuss what positively and negatively affects our mental health

- Further understand the definition of a young carer

- Explore feelings that young carers may experience

- Identify ways in which young carers can be supported

Activity

This lesson can be used as a follow-up to Activity 25. Begin by asking the children to reflect upon the role of a young carer. Pose the question: What do you know and understand about the role of a young carer? Provide the children with an opportunity to use the "What is a young carer?" resource to highlight what these roles might be.

Further explore the associated feelings connected with these roles to help children to develop compassion and empathy for young carers. Provide the children with the feeling cards resource. Their task is to put them in order from the feelings that they think the young carer experiences the most, to the least. They need to be able to justify and provide a reason for their choices and explain how this could change – this can be recorded alongside the associated role.

Explain that although you know it is hard to see someone you love suffering or needing help and that many young carers will find it difficult to cope from time to time; providing support, listening and being there for a young carer will help them to feel positive and better about themselves.

Questions for thinking

- What is a young carer?
- What types of things might a young carer do to help take care of someone?
- How do you think this makes a young carer feel and why?
- What can you do to support a young carer?

Resources

- Feeling cards
- What is a young carer?

What is a young carer?

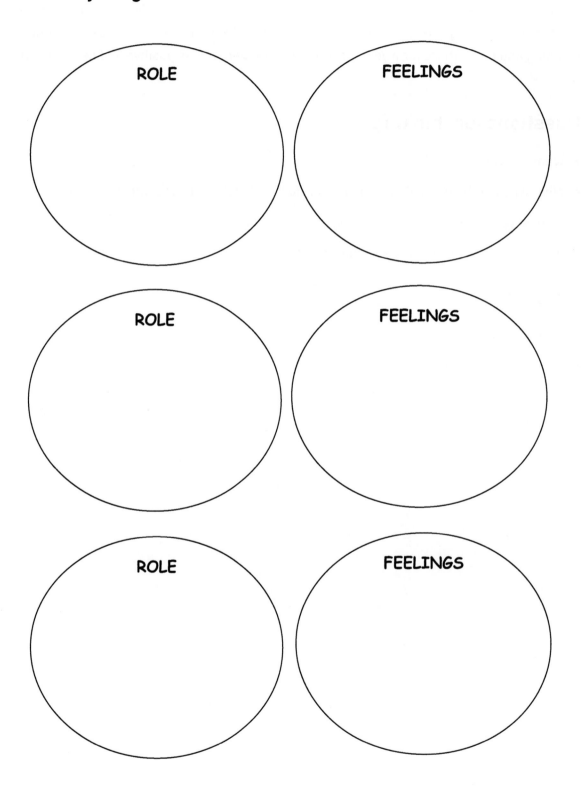

ROLE

FEELINGS

ROLE

FEELINGS

ROLE

FEELINGS

Feeling words

Angry	Hopeful	Sad
Happy	Excited	Worried
Stressed	Annoyed	Compassionate
Bored	Jealous	Tired
Surprised	Kind	Scared
Confident	Disappointed	Ashamed
Depressed	Nervous	Loved
Lonely	Proud	Embarrassed

PART VI

COPING WITH LOSS AND EXCLUSION

The resources in this section provide children with an opportunity to identify feelings associated with feeling left out and the negative impact of exclusion due to individual differences, e.g. race, gender or disability. The children will also think about the feelings associated with bereavement.

Activity 27

LEFT OUT AND FORGOTTEN

Age: 8–11

Context

Children could experience some form of exclusion throughout their lives either at home or at school. This might involve feeling left out within a friendship circle or not being included in a game. Even the arrival of a baby brother or sister could have an impact on a young person, especially if they feel they are now receiving less attention, or they think they are cared for less than before. The feeling of exclusion can result in resentment, upset and frustration and can have an impact on behaviour as well as social, emotional and mental wellbeing.

Learning outcomes

The children will have an opportunity to:

- Identify the feelings of those who might feel left out

- Show empathy towards those who feel excluded

- Identify strategies to help someone manage negative feelings

- Discuss what can be done to ensure people feel included

Activity

This activity provides children with an opportunity to discuss, develop empathy and an understanding for those that might feel left out and what they can do to help. Explain to the children that they are going to be thinking about feelings associated with being left out or excluded. Pose the questions: What does excluded mean? Have you ever felt left out of anything? How did this make you feel? Take feedback from the class.

Read out the poem titled "Feeling left out" and use the questions for thinking to encourage children to infer and reason. Following that, ask the children to generate a concept map of feeling words associated with how that person might be feeling. This could be done in pairs or in small groups. Additionally, ask them to identify what they would do to help this person manage how they are feeling, the impact of exclusion and what they would do to make them feel included.

Questions for thinking

- How is this person feeling?

- What do you think this person can do to help them manage how they are feeling?

- What do you think could have happened to make them feel this way?

- What solutions could you provide this person to help them feel better?

- What would you do to make them feel included?

Resources

- Poem – Feeling left out

Feeling left out

Left Out

Forgotten

Excluded

This is what I am.

Always the last one to be remembered,

The last one to be cared for

And the last to be picked for the football team.

I guess I am not that important

I guess I am not that good.

Left Out

Forgotten

Excluded

This is what I am.

Activity 28

FEELING LEFT OUT

Age: 7–11

Context

Children might feel lonely or afraid if they feel that someone is treating them unfairly. This can impact upon their mood and behaviours, resulting in frustration or upset – they may not know what to do. Social anxiety can occur if children feel that they are being made to feel disconnected from others. Creating an environment that encourages children to talk openly about how they are feeling will help them to manage their emotions and seek solutions.

Learning outcomes

The children will have an opportunity to:

- Identify the feelings of those who might feel left out due to individual difference

- Show empathy towards those who feel excluded

- Identify strategies to help someone manage negative feelings

- Discuss what can be done to ensure people feel included

Activity

This lesson provides an alternative activity to help children discuss and understand the feelings associated with feeling left out with a focus on seeking help. Pose the questions: What does it mean to feel left out? Can you provide examples? Invite children to provide examples that are personal and meaningful to them. Explore how this made them feel and what they did to help them feel better.

Ask the children to create a poster that illustrates the importance of integration and inclusion. The poster should explore the negative impact of being excluded and outline the importance of seeking help. They might consider different strategies that could be used such as talking to a friend, speaking to a teacher or writing it down. The feeling cards resource can be used to stimulate discussion around associated feelings.

Questions for thinking

- What feelings are associated with being left out?

- What does integration mean?

- What can someone do if they feel left out?

- What can you do if you see someone being excluded?

Resources

- Feeling words

- Feeling left out poster (template)

Feeling words

Angry	Hopeful	Sad
Happy	Excited	Worried
Stressed	Annoyed	Compassionate
Bored	Jealous	Tired
Surprised	Kind	Scared
Confident	Disappointed	Ashamed
Depressed	Nervous	Loved
Lonely	Proud	Embarrassed

Feeling left out poster (template)

Activity 29

LUCIANA AND HER GRANDMA

Age: 7–11

Context

Children who have been bereaved by the death of someone will cope in different ways and although schools can be a busy place, it is important that those affected know that they are listened to and have someone to talk to or a safe place to go to so that they can simply be themselves.

Learning outcomes

The children will have an opportunity to:

- Understand good and not so good feelings and associated language

- Recognise that they may experience conflicting emotions

- Identify a range of feelings associated with loss of a loved one

- Understand that everyone will express feelings in different ways

- Recognise how to show support and show empathy towards someone experiencing loss of a loved one

Activity

This activity will allow children to identify with a range of feelings associated with loss and an opportunity to illustrate empathy and support. You may wish to sit the children in a horseshoe shape to begin this session. Due to the sensitive nature of this topic it will be important to ensure that children are made to feel comfortable, understand that it is a safe space and it is ok if they do not want to share.

Explain to the children that they are going to be hearing a story about a young girl called Luciana whose grandma has passed away. Bereavement will look different for the individuals within your class determined by culture. It could be beneficial to explore this and explain that many people experience grief and a sense of loss after the death of a loved one. But the way in which they experience and express these feelings will differ.

Whilst reading the story, ask the children to think about how Luciana is feeling and why. Following the story, use the questions for thinking to guide discussion.

Use a hand puppet or soft toy as Luciana and encourage the children to ask Luciana questions about her relationship with her grandma. Follow-up with a discussion on how the children can help Luciana manage how she is feeling – this can be recorded on a concept map.

Questions for thinking

- Why do you think Luciana has been in trouble at school since her grandma passed away?
- Who do you think can help her at school?
- Her friends no longer want to play with her – what could her friends do to help?
- How do you think Luciana is coping with the passing of her grandma?

Resources

- Luciana and her grandma

Luciana and her grandma

Luciana has been feeling terribly sad recently.

Last week her grandma, who she would see every weekend, passed away due to coronavirus.

Her grandma was 75 years old and had a heart condition which meant that she found it difficult to breathe.

Every Sunday Luciana would visit her in her care home.

She was a loving and very special person.

Luciana enjoyed playing games with her grandma, eating chocolate cake and singing songs.

Since her grandma passed away Luciana has not been completing her homework and has had several arguments with her friends at school.

Her friends no longer include her in their games, and she feels left out and lonely.

Luciana is beginning to make up excuses for missing school.

"Mum, I have a tummy ache today."

"Mum, my head hurts."

Her mum is worried about Luciana and wants to meet her teacher, Mr Anderson, to find a way of helping Luciana manage how she is feeling about the loss of her grandma.

Activity 30

MY SPECIAL PERSON

Age: 7–11

Context

Children who experience bereavement will need support in how to manage how they are feeling. Every situation is different, and the wellbeing of children will be affected depending on the circumstances of the death and the nature of the relationship they had with the person who has died.

Learning outcomes

The children will have an opportunity to:

- Understand good and not so good feelings and associated language

- Identify a range of feelings associated with loss of a loved one

- Understand that everyone will express feelings in different ways

- Recognise how to show support and empathy towards someone experiencing loss of a loved one

- Be able to talk about loss and how it made them feel

Activity

This activity will allow children to talk about loss, whether this is a friend, family member or a pet. Tell the children that they are going to be talking about things that might cause sadness, but that's ok. Explain that you would like them to think about the things that made this person special. You may wish to provide the children with an example.

For example, my cat Anna-Marie passed away a few months ago. She had beautiful blue eyes that would brighten up my day. Every morning, she would quietly come into my room, jump onto my bed and purr, wanting me to stroke her. I miss her terribly.

The children can use the "My special person" resource to reflect and think about their special person and the things that they shared together that made them happy.

Questions for thinking

- Who is your special person?

- What makes this person special to you?

- What did you share with this person that makes you happy?

- How can talking about your feelings help you?

- What else can you do to help you manage how you are feeling?

Resources

- My special person

My special person

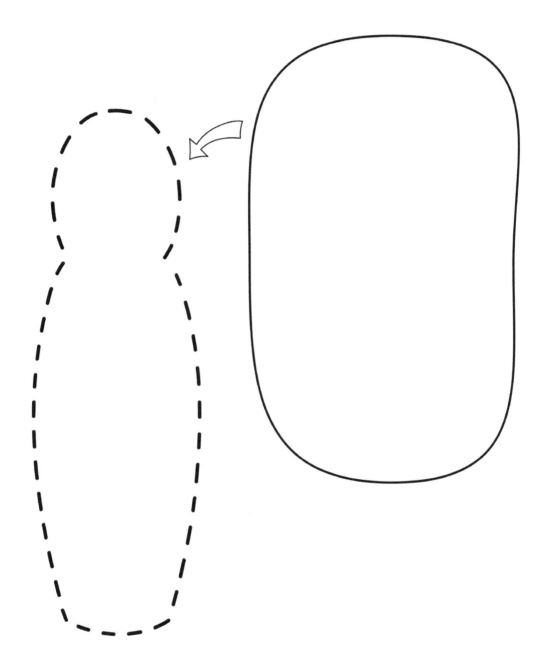

My special person

My special person

PART VII

RESILIENCE

The resources in this section provide children with an opportunity to identify strategies to help build resilience using a resilience toolbox and role models such as the first Black self-made millionaire, Madam C J Walker, and Paralympic Powerlifter Ali Jawad.

Activity 31

RESILIENCE TOOLBOX

Age: 7–11

Context

Resilient children can resist adversity, cope with uncertainty and recover more successfully from traumatic events or episodes (Newham, 2002). Learning practical ways to help young people build resilience will help them to manage the complexities of life using a variety of strategies to problem-solve. Schools are in a unique place to help to contribute to healthy attitudes and self-awareness in young people. Promoting resilience in young people can lead to better outcomes academically, socially and emotionally.

Learning outcomes

The children will have an opportunity to:

- Understand the definition of resilience

- Understand the benefits of developing resilience

- Identify strategies to develop resilience

- Explore positive and negative emotions associated with building resilience

Activity

Explain that the term resilience is the ability to manage challenges and overcome obstacles that we may face in our everyday lives. Write on the board: Resilience is the ability to manage adversity regardless of individual difference. Open discussion on what this means to them, including their understanding of individual difference.

It is important that children recognise that everyone should be provided with an opportunity to succeed. In building resilience, the learning environment, the developing of relationships and the differentiation of strategies in enabling all learners to grow are important parts of resisting any unconscious biases that could prevent a child from reaching their academic potential.

The stories of resilience in Activities 32 and 33 can be used to engage children in reflection and analysis, looking at the tools used by Madam C J Walker and Ali Jawad that helped them to overcome adverse circumstances. Ask the children to use the "My resilience toolbox" resource to write down the tools that they use currently, in addition to new strategies that they will try, to help them when they are faced with challenges.

Questions for thinking

- What does resilience mean to you?
- What do you understand by individual difference?
- What strategies do you currently use to help you to build resilience?
- What new strategies could you add to your toolbox?

Resources

- My resilience toolbox

My resilience toolbox

Activity 32

MADAM C J WALKER

Age: 8–11

Context

Madam C J Walker, whose birthname was Sarah Breedlove, was born to parents who had been slaves. An American entrepreneur who created specialised hair products for African American hair, she made history by becoming the first American woman to become a self-made millionaire. Her journey to building her company is one of determination, desire and resilience.

Learning outcomes

The children will have an opportunity to:

- Learn about the life of Madam C J Walker

- Identify the challenges faced by Madam C J Walker

- Identify the impact of unfair treatment on emotional health

- Illustrate compassion and develop empathy for others

- Find solutions for negative situations to create change

Activity

This activity will teach children about Madam C J Walker, America's first female self-made millionaire. The children will have the opportunity to learn about her inspiration, the challenges that she faced and what she did to help her overcome them. Explain to the children that they are going to explore the life of Madam C J Walker who was America's first self-made millionaire.

Tell the children that Madam C J Walker suffered from hair loss due to a scalp condition. This made her feel very self-conscious and embarrassed. She didn't think that she was as pretty as others and would cover her head to hide her hair loss. She was always judged for her

Madam C J Walker

dark skin, told that she was worthless and finally, had enough of it. This is what inspired her to do something about it and that she did by creating and building her business making hair products. She was able to help her own hair and help others too.

Read out the "Madam C J Walker" story and ask the children to think about the challenges that she might have faced and what she did to overcome these challenges. Use the questions for thinking to guide discussion encouraging children to think critically, analyse and provide a reason for their thinking.

Questions for thinking

- Who was Madam C J Walker?

- What have you learned about her journey to becoming a self-made millionaire?

- Can you identify some of the challenges that she might have faced?

- How did she overcome these challenges?

- Can you identify growth mindset statements that you would associate with Madam C J Walker?

Resources

- Madam C J Walker

Madam C J Walker

How much work does it take to make a million dollars? How much time, sweat and tears go into building something that'll last and make that much money? All while being treated unfairly and facing prejudice for being a Black woman?

It takes everything a person has, from their heart to their mind – it takes a lot of grit, desire and persistence. Madam C J Walker did it in a time in America when being a Black woman meant having fewer rights and opportunities, in a time when being Black meant that you were worthless and held with low regard.

Who was Madam C J Walker? She was a woman with a dream, who invented hair products for women and popularised the hot comb. Her real name was Sarah Breedlove. She was born on a plantation in Louisiana only two years after the Civil War, in 1867. Her parents had been slaves.

Sarah worked in cotton fields with her sister when she was young. And then became a mother. Finally, after moving to St. Louis, young Sarah would join the African Methodist Episcopal Church, where she was introduced to many successful Black people who would inspire her to do great things.

After a troubled marriage, Sarah would set off to work for herself. She was also facing terrible hair loss and felt embarrassed about the way that she looked and would often try to cover her head. She discovered Annie Turbo Malone's "The Great Wonderful Hair Grower." This worked wonders and filled Sarah with joy as her hair began to grow. She eventually became a saleswoman but working for someone else didn't sit right with Sarah.

Sarah wanted something more and something to call her own. So, she decided to say goodbye to Sarah Breedlove and created her own brand. Sarah became Madam C J Walker and made her own line of hair care products for Black women. This was no easy task and required a lot of hard work, long days and early mornings. Madam C J Walker faced many setbacks, with people actively trying to stop her from succeeding. But she was determined to not let anyone stand in her way and find a way of not only helping herself, but helping others too.

Madam C J Walker knew something deep in her heart: To succeed, you needed to lift others. So, she moved to Indianapolis, where she built a factory and started training programmes. All across America, she created a workforce of saleswomen who would introduce her product to new customers. This was called the Walker System. Her advertising also kept many Black newspapers afloat, by making enough money to stay open during troubled times.

All across the United States, Central America and even the Caribbean, Madam C J. Walker employed men and women who sold her products. She employed thousands and became America's first Black American woman self-made millionaire.

But she didn't settle on her own success, she wanted to give back to the Black communities that bought and believed in her products. She herself thought "cleanliness and loveliness" was a way to help others and lift their spirits. And even though she lived in a big mansion, she never stopped supporting people. She gave lots of money to organisations and charities to help the Black community. She wanted to leave a legacy, and that she did.

Activity 33

ALI JAWAD

Age: 8–11

Context

British Paralympic Powerlifter Ali Jawad was born without legs and took up powerlifting at the age of 16 years old. He was born in Lebanon; however, in his early life, conflict broke out between Lebanon and Israel, resulting in Ali and his family migrating to England with fear of war. When his family arrived in England, they had very little and didn't speak any English which they found very challenging. Despite this, Ali had found a safehaven in England and a love for sport.

Learning outcomes

The children will have an opportunity to:

- Learn about the life of Ali Jawad

- Identify the challenges faced by Ali Jawad

- Recognise how resilience can help to overcome challenges

- Identify the impact of unfair treatment on emotional health

- Illustrate compassion and develop empathy for others

- Find solutions for negative situations to create change

Activity

Ali Jawad's highs and lows of his sporting career and personal health will provide children with an opportunity to explore strength in character, leading a healthy lifestyle and the importance of having a positive attitude.

Explain to the children that they are going to explore the life of Ali Jawad, a Paralympic Powerlifter. Pose the question: Do you know what a powerlifter does? What is the difference between the Olympics and Paralympics?

Use the Ali Jawad resource to talk through key life experiences and ask the children to reflect upon Ali Jawad's strength in character and determination and how he used his experiences to help him overcome difficult situations.

Following that, use the "My healthy lifestyle" resource to ask children to think about what they do to lead a healthy lifestyle and how leading a healthy lifestyle can improve their mental health.

Questions for thinking

- What have you learned about Ali Jawad?
- What challenges did he face growing up?
- What were his experiences like at school?
- What tools do you think he used to help him overcome challenges?
- What do you do to lead a healthy lifestyle?

Resources

- My healthy lifestyle
- Ali Jawad

My healthy lifestyle

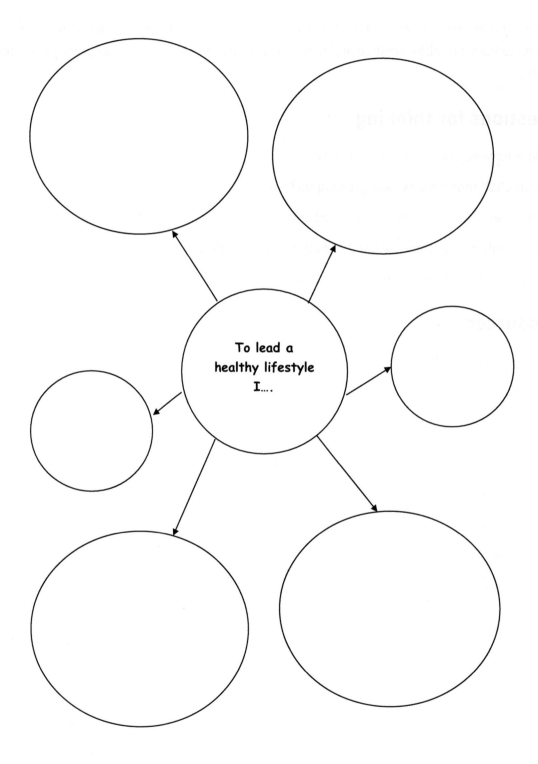

To lead a
healthy lifestyle
I....

Ali Jawad

Ali Jawad was born in Lebanon without legs.

Ali enjoyed school, was popular and always felt included.

Ali liked playing lots of different sports. As a teenager he tried Judo before finding his calling in powerlifting.

He migrated to England with his family with fear of war.

At the age of only 19 Ali was diagnosed with Crohns disease, a lifelong illness. He had to undertake a life-threatening operation and everyone thought his Paralympic dream was over .

As an amputee Ali used his arms as legs and had to learn to find ways to lift himself up.

He competed at the London 2010 Paralympics and finished 4th due to a judging error.

He continued to work hard and won gold in the 2014 World Championships and a year later, gold in the European Championships.

The first time Ali went to the gym he had lifted 100KG!

Only 4 months after his operation he started to train and finished 5th at the 2010 Common Wealth Games. It was like a miracle.

PART VIII

ANXIETY AND DEPRESSION

The resources in this section provide children with an opportunity to recognise symptoms of depression and identify the things that make them worry. They will also look at what causes fear of failure and strategies to overcome this, such as managing exam pressure, or moving to a new school and managing a new environment.

Activity 34

WHAT IS DEPRESSION?

Age: 9–11

Context

Children can feel sad, upset and a little low sometimes. This will be determined by their life experiences. Perhaps things didn't go their way, they might be feeling hurt or have been bereaved which can cause an expression of negative emotions. Depression however is more than just being sad or upset. Depression affects the way children think, and how they see themselves and their future. Along with feeling sad or irritable, children may feel that nothing is worthwhile and that things will never get better.

Learning outcomes

The children will have an opportunity to:

- Be able to talk about and respond to a range of feelings

- Understand the definition of depression

- Recognise signs and symptoms of depression

- Recognise when to ask for support

- Recognise how to support others

Activity

This activity provides children with an opportunity to explore what depression looks like and how it can make people feel. Pose the question: What do you understand by depression? Generate discussion around depression thinking about what the children already know.

Explain to the children that depression affects the way that they think, feel and behave. Depression can stop them enjoying the things they normally like doing or taking part in their usual activities. Generate a word amnesty looking at the words that the children would associate with depression and ask them to provide a reason why.

Use the "What is depression?" resource to explore signs and symptoms of depression. For each, ask the children to provide strategies of support. Explain that it is really important to talk to their friend if they notice that don't seem themselves, listen to what they have to say and that it is ok to ask for help.

Questions for thinking

- What does depression mean to you?

- How do you know if someone is depressed?

- What can you do to support someone who is depressed?

Resources

- What is depression?

What is depression?

Feeling lonely	Can't get out of bed	Loss of a loved one	Feeling as though no-one takes you seriously
Parents are arguing	Don't feel like having fun with your friends	Moving house	Going to a new school
Feeling rejected	Comparing yourself to others	Feeling sad all the time	Being bullied
Pressure to always do well	Feeling left out	Feeling like you cant do anything right	Lack of friends
Feeling anxious or afraid	Feeling constantly judged by others	Finding it difficult to sleep	Lack of support from others
Feeling helpless	Lack of friends	Feeling as thought no one cares	Parental separation

Activity 35

WORRYING

Age: 8–11

Context

A build-up of frustrations and disappointments can cause children to worry. It is important to encourage children to notice what makes them feel anxious and guide them to finding possible solutions. Providing comfort, reassurance and keeping things in perspective can all help children to manage big feelings.

Learning outcomes

The children will have an opportunity to:

- Be able to talk about and respond to a range of feelings

- Recognise signs and symptoms of depression

- Recognise when to ask for support

- Recognise how to support others

Activity

This activity provides children with an opportunity to explore the things that make them worry and what they can do to help them manage negative or big feelings. Pose the question: What types of things make you worry? Ask the children to think about what causes this worry and how it makes them feel.

Explain to the children that worrying about something can cause stress and this worry in their minds can affect how they feel, how they think and how they behave. Talking about their problems can help to release any negative emotions and find solutions.

Ask the children to use the "What am I worried about?" resource to write down the things that make them worry. Writing things down and talking through them will not only help to release any negative tension but allow them to gain new insight on the situation that is causing them the problem. It will help them to find out that they are not alone and there might be others who share the same or similar worries.

Questions for thinking

- What things make you worry?
- How does worrying make you feel?
- What can you do to manage big feelings?

Resources

- What am I worried about?

What am I worried about?

Activity 36

JASMINE'S FEAR OF FAILURE (I)

Age: 7–11

Context

Children are expressing a fear of failure at increasingly younger ages. As some prepare to take tests and exams, many schools have reported an increase in emotional wellbeing issues amongst their pupils. High expectations can be internally driven by children themselves as well as external pressure from parents or the school itself. It is important that children have the opportunity to share personal experiences and how resilience can help them to manage adversities in our everchanging world.

Learning outcomes

The children will have an opportunity to:

- Recognise how to develop and use a growth mindset

- Recognise what causes the fear of failure

- Identify strategies for coping with the fear of failure

- Provide solutions for managing negative feelings

Activity

Ask the children to consider the things that may cause fear and then further explore the relationship this has with the fear of trying something new. Pose the questions: Who enjoys trying new things? Ask the children to reflect on the reason why and the traits, characteristics or tools that help them to try things, even if they may find it daunting or difficult.

Tell the children that they are going to learn about a young girl called Jasmine who has a wonderful opportunity to join a professional girls' football team. Pose the question: How do you think Jasmine must be feeling?

Read the story "Jasmine's fear" and use it to stimulate discussion on fear of failure, guided by the questions for thinking. Encourage children to relate this experience to that of their own or other situations such as taking a school test, riding a bike for the first time or starting a new sports club.

Questions for thinking

- Can you identify how Jasmine is feeling?

- Why do you think Jasmine feels this way?

- How do you know, what evidence do you have?

- Who can Jasmine talk to about how she is feeling?

Resources

- Jasmine's fear

Jasmine's fear

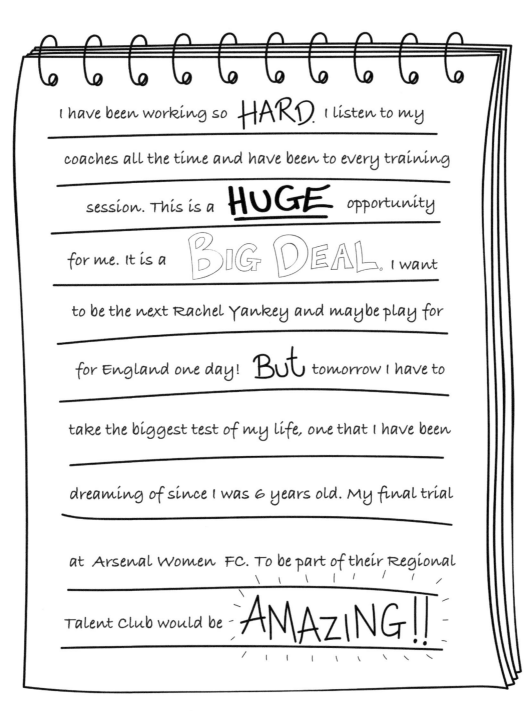

I have been working so HARD. I listen to my coaches all the time and have been to every training session. This is a HUGE opportunity for me. It is a BIG DEAL. I want to be the next Rachel Yankey and maybe play for for England one day! But tomorrow I have to take the biggest test of my life, one that I have been dreaming of since I was 6 years old. My final trial at Arsenal Women FC. To be part of their Regional Talent Club would be AMAZING!!

Activity 37

JASMINE'S FEAR OF FAILURE (II)

Age: 7–11

Context

The fear of failure can stop children from moving forward to achieve their ambitions and goals. By helping children to recognise how their mindset can help them overcome their fears, in addition to helping them use experiences of failing as opportunities to learn, children will be more willing to persevere and try, even if something seems challenging.

Those with fear of failure often experience fatigue and low energy, they feel emotionally drained and are more dissatisfied with their lives. This can negatively impact upon their academic performance and behaviours, affecting their friends and overall happiness.

Learning outcomes

The children will have an opportunity to:

- Reflect on how to develop and use a growth mindset

- Recognise what causes the fear of failure

- Identify strategies for coping with the fear of failure

- Provide solutions for managing negative feelings

Activity

This lesson can be used as a follow-up to Activity 36. Ask the children to reflect on Jasmine's story. Pose the question: What did you learn about Jasmine? Considerations for the discussion are:

- What does Jasmine most enjoy?

- How do you know this?

- What is Jasmine worried about?

- Why do you think this might be?

The "Jasmine's mindset" resource can be used to illustrate the expression of negative emotions, including anxiety, caused by a fear of failing. Discuss solutions that the children can provide Jasmine to help her to develop a growth mindset and the resilience to manage her situation. Ask the children to write a middle and ending to the story Jasmine's fear, which describes the strategies that she used whilst on trial, the outcome of the trial and how this made her feel.

Questions for thinking

- How can you help Jasmine overcome her fear of failure?
- How do you think growth mindset tools will help Jasmine in the future?
- Who can Jasmine talk to about how she is feeling?
- Is Jasmine able to go through with her trial?
- What is the outcome of her trial?
- What happens next?

Resources

- Jasmine's mindset

Jasmine's mindset

Activity 38

EXAM PRESSURE

Age: 9–11

Context

There is an increasing number of children who are suffering from exam-related stress and teachers are reporting that this is becoming an increasing problem in schools. Pressure of exams can be a cause of anxiety, one of the most common diagnosable mental health conditions among children. The possibility of failing is deeply worrying for children. Many children worry that they will disappoint their teachers or parents if they perform badly in exams.

Learning outcomes

The children will have an opportunity to:

- Be able to talk about and respond to a range of feelings

- Recognise signs and symptoms of anxiety

- Recognise when to ask for support

- Recognise how to manage big feelings

Activity

This activity provides children with an opportunity to explore feelings associated with exams and tests. Pose the question: How do exams or tests make you feel? Why? What do you do to help you manage exam stress?

Whilst for some children taking tests can be a stressful experience, for others it might be something that they thrive from. It is important to help children recognise that the feelings that they experience will be different for any given situation. For children who view exams as a challenge and something that they are afraid of, it is important to explore why and how they manage under pressure.

Read the poem "My brain is like a ball of string" and invite children to consider how taking an exam made the child feel and what advice they can provide to help the child to overcome their anxieties. Through the poem, explore why children express negative emotions as a result of exams.

Questions for thinking

- How do exams make you feel?

- Why do they make you feel this way?

- What can you do to help you manage stress as a result of exams?

Resources

- Poem – My brain is like a ball of string

My brain is like a ball of string

I studied hard and made some notes.
I learned the dates and all the quotes.
With every book, I took my time
to understand and underline.
And when I didn't get the rule,
I raised the problem back at school.
And asked the teacher to explain.
Then, if in doubt, I asked again.

I listened hard in every class,
and tried at least to get a pass.
I did my homework, day and night;
got almost every answer right.
I didn't see my friends. Instead,
I stayed inside my house and read.
On weekends at the library,
the only kid around was me.
And no, it wasn't too much fun.
But work is work and must be done.
Tomorrow is the big exam.
And am I ready? Yes, I am.

Okay, the big exam day's here.
But why am I so full of fear?
I studied just the way I should.
And yesterday I felt so good.
I knew the things I had to know.
So, where'd that information go?
I can't recall a single thing.
My brain is like a ball of string.
It's tangled up in crazy knots,
like I've completely lost the plot.

The facts and figures in my mind,
are somehow very hard to find.
The names are like a mystery,
as if they're ancient history.
And all the stuff I memorised?
Completely gone, to my surprise.
The cupboard in my head is bare.
I'm searching, but there's nothing there.
It's like a nightmare in the day.
I need to wake up right away.

And now I'm heading to the room.
I'm walking down the path of doom.
It's time for my examination;
a terrifying situation.
My hands are damp with clammy sweat.
My mouth is dry as it can get.
I'm feeling faint. My head is light.
I bunch my fists up really tight.
I'm breathing hard. I start to shake.
I've also got a stomach ache.
My heart is pounding in my chest.
I guess you'd say I'm pretty stressed.

I glance around me at my mates.
They're looking in a similar state.
They mutter, fidget, walk around.
Or stare ahead without a sound.
They're gripped with panic just like me.
We're suffering from anxiety.
It started small but grew and grew.
This isn't fair, what can we do?

Activity 39

A NEW ENVIRONMENT

Age: 9–11

Context

A new environment can be a daunting experience for children, causing stress, anxiety and worry. Leaving familiarities, security and comfort behind such as friends and family, can be lonely, and for some children a negative experience. Teaching children to build resilience to overcome adversities, including change, will help them to develop coping skills to not only manage big feelings, but have the confidence to create and develop new relationships.

Learning outcomes

The children will have an opportunity to:

- Be able to talk about and respond to a range of feelings

- Recognise signs and symptoms of anxiety

- Recognise when to ask for support

- Recognise how to manage big feelings

Activity

This activity provides children with an opportunity to explore feelings associated with moving home, resulting in having to attend a new school. Pose the questions: Can you think of a time where you have attended something new for the first time? This might include a new sports club, visiting a dentist for the first time or even trying a new experience. Ask children to think about how this made them feel and give reasons why they felt this way.

Explain that they will all experience something new at some point in their lives and this can cause a range of feelings and emotions. Tell the children that they are going to hear a story about a young boy called Lucas who has moved home and as a result, has to attend a new school. Ask them to consider how Lucas is feeling about attending his new school and evidence in the story that provides them with this information.

Read the story "Lucas and his new school" and invite the children to consider what Lucas can do to help him manage his big feelings. The children can plan and write a diary where Lucas reflects upon his first day in his new school.

Questions for thinking

- How is Lucas feeling about moving house?
- What does he miss and how do you know?
- How was Lucas feeling about attending his new school?
- What evidence in the story suggests that he was apprehensive?

Resources

- Lucas and his new school
- Dear Diary

Lucas and his new school

Lucas glanced around the room in the early morning light. The curtains and wallpaper were different. The wardrobe was different. The desk and chair were the same, but not in the same place.

He rolled on his side and looked at his bedside clock. The red digits blinked back at him. 7.15 a.m. In a few minutes, the alarm would go off, and he'd hardly slept a wink all night.

"You'll be fine," his mum had said as they'd sat drinking chocolate milk in their new kitchen. "It's just another school. You'll soon make friends."

Lucas had nodded and smiled. He knew how proud his parents were of their new house. And it was nice. He had a larger room, and the garden was bigger. But it just wasn't home.

He liked his old neighbourhood, where he knew everyone, and everyone knew him. He liked his old school, with his old teachers, like Mr Clarke, who gave him a cool handshake every time they met. But most of all he missed his friends. Shanaya, Brad, Devinda and Bela. They'd all grown up together. And sure, they'd keep in touch, but it wasn't the same. They weren't round the corner like they used to be.

Lucas sighed and stared at the ceiling. Inside, he had a bad case of the "What Ifs."

What if he didn't like his new school? What if he couldn't find his way around? What if the teachers didn't like him? What if the work was too hard? What if the football team was too good and he couldn't get on it? Worst of all, what if he didn't make any friends? What if the kids here made fun of his accent, or his trainers, or his haircut, or whatever?

Lucas buried his face in his pillow and shouted, "I don't want to go!" just as the alarm began buzzing.

But he had to go, and he knew it. And an hour later, he was outside the school in his dad's car being dropped off.

"Go on, son," his dad said. "Best foot forward. You're going to love it."

Lucas took a deep breath and got out of the car.

For a moment, he stood there, watching as a crowd of kids streamed up the driveway towards the glass-panelled school.

"Okay," said Lucas, hoisting his backpack onto his shoulder. "This is it!"

Dear Diary

Dear Diary...

PART IX

RACE, RELIGION AND CULTURE

The resources in this section provide children with an opportunity to understand the definition of a refugee and understand the lives of celebrity refugees. They will also look at the definition of Islamophobia, prejudice and explore the Black Lives Matter movement and its significance to not only Black heritage, but to society as a whole.

Activity 40

LIFE OF A REFUGEE (I)

Age: 8–11

Context

Many children and families have arrived in the UK as migrants or refugees escaping war or devastation in their home countries. Children may have friends that have experienced such torment and equally, teachers may be working within a school demographic with a migrant or refugee population. Such experiences can have an impact on social and emotional wellbeing.

Learning outcomes

The children will have an opportunity to:

- Understand the definition of a migrant and refugee

- Recognise why people migrate

- Reflect upon the impact of migration on children and their families

- Show empathy towards those who have fled their home country to create a better life

- Discuss how migration can impact upon mental and emotional health

Activity

This activity provides children with an opportunity to discuss, develop empathy for and an understanding of those who have left their home and what they can do to help. Tell the children that they are going to be thinking about feelings associated with those that have had to leave their home country because of fear due to war.

Explain that people who leave their home country to seek a better life somewhere else because of war or devastation are called refugees. They leave because it is unsafe for them to live where they are, so they look for safety and shelter somewhere else. Moving to another country is called migration. This is where people look to settle somewhere else.

Pose the questions: Have you heard of the term "refugee" before? What do you understand about migrants and refugees? Take feedback from the class and make a note of any misconceptions as this may lead to further work.

Read out the story "Hamid's journey to England" and use this as a basis for group discussion for this activity.

Questions for thinking

- How do you feel about Hamid's story? What was the saddest or most shocking part of the story? How might you feel in Hamid's situation?

- Close your eyes, can you imagine what it must have been like for Hamid in Afghanistan? What can you hear? What can you see?

- When they left in secret, what do you think they took with them? What would you have taken with you and why?

- Why do you think it is important for us to know about the experiences of migrants and refugees?

Resources

- Hamid's journey to England

Hamid's journey to England

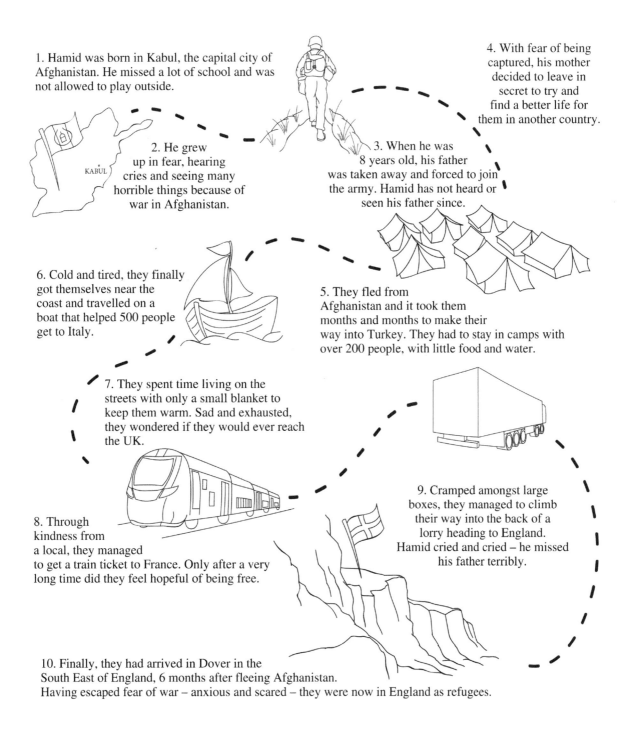

1. Hamid was born in Kabul, the capital city of Afghanistan. He missed a lot of school and was not allowed to play outside.

2. He grew up in fear, hearing cries and seeing many horrible things because of war in Afghanistan.

KABUL

3. When he was 8 years old, his father was taken away and forced to join the army. Hamid has not heard or seen his father since.

4. With fear of being captured, his mother decided to leave in secret to try and find a better life for them in another country.

5. They fled from Afghanistan and it took them months and months to make their way into Turkey. They had to stay in camps with over 200 people, with little food and water.

6. Cold and tired, they finally got themselves near the coast and travelled on a boat that helped 500 people get to Italy.

7. They spent time living on the streets with only a small blanket to keep them warm. Sad and exhausted, they wondered if they would ever reach the UK.

8. Through kindness from a local, they managed to get a train ticket to France. Only after a very long time did they feel hopeful of being free.

9. Cramped amongst large boxes, they managed to climb their way into the back of a lorry heading to England. Hamid cried and cried – he missed his father terribly.

10. Finally, they had arrived in Dover in the South East of England, 6 months after fleeing Afghanistan. Having escaped fear of war – anxious and scared – they were now in England as refugees.

Activity 41

LIFE OF A REFUGEE (II)

Age: 8–11

Context

Refugee children may become separated from their parents, siblings and relatives whilst fleeing their home to find safety. Alone in a new country, they have to try to rebuild a new life, without the love and support of family and friends. They may have experienced extreme torture and bring those experiences and memories with them, whilst trying to find somewhere safe to live. A new environment, a series of traumatic experiences and fear can all contribute towards their mental health.

Learning outcomes

The children will have an opportunity to:

- Reflect upon the definition of a migrant and refugee

- Recognise why people migrate

- Reflect upon the impact of migration on children and their families

- Show empathy towards those who have fled their home country to create a better life

- Discuss how migration can impact upon mental and emotional health

- Recognise why migrants and refugees are treated unfairly

Activity

This lesson provides an extension to Activity 40. Ask children to reflect upon the definition of a refugee and migrant. Tell the children that unfortunately, migrants can be seen in a negative light due to stereotyping. Invite them to research celebrities who are migrants. The following questions could be used to guide their research:

- What is their heritage and background?

- Where did they migrate from and why?

- What challenges have they faced?

- How have they overcome these challenges?

- What do they do now?

The "News" template can be used for children to create their news report. Some examples of refugee celebrities include:

- Rita Ora – singer

- Saido Berahino – footballer

- Victor Moses – footballer

- Michael Marks – Founder, Marks & Spencer

Questions for thinking

- Who did you research and why?

- What did you find out?

- What have you learned?

- How will you use this learning?

Resources

- In the news

In the news

Written by . . . .

Activity 42

PSYCHOLOGICAL IMPACT OF ISLAMOPHOBIA (I)

Age: 9–11

Context

Children learn morals, values and beliefs from their family, peers, teachers, the media and others around them. The influence from this socialisation informs their view of the world and their view of others. This can lead to stereotypes and prejudiced views of individuals and groups of people. The way in which they treat others as a result of these views can have an impact on the emotional health of the victim.

Learning outcomes

The children will have an opportunity to:

- Understand the definition of prejudice

- Understand the definition of Islamophobia

- Recognise how their behaviours can affect others

- Explore feelings and emotions associated with prejudice

- Recognise factors that can influence thought and behaviour

Activity

Explain that the term prejudice means judging someone or having an idea about them before you actually know anything about them. It can also mean having an opinion about something without knowing anything about it. Open discussion on what the children already understand about prejudice, what it means to them and what they would do to get to know someone or learn more about someone, e.g. their background, heritage, culture, likes or dislikes.

Explain that unfortunately, some people are treated unfairly and judged based on what they look like and in this session, the children will explore prejudice against people who are

Muslim. This is known as Islamophobia, which is the fear of Islam. Children may already be aware of incidents involving Islamophobia and the misconception that Islam is a violent ideology rather than a religion. It is important that work around this subject is done before completing this lesson.

The following discussion points could be used to explore the causes of Islamophobia:

- Ignorance – a lack of understanding which can be combated with knowledge and understanding

- Terrorism – international politics, specifically linked to Islam and targeting Muslims

The "Headline news" resource will provide the children with an opportunity to illustrate empathy, discuss and identify the impressions that the headlines give of Muslims and explore the negative impact that prejudice and stereotyping can have on emotional health.

Questions for thinking

- What is Islamophobia?

- What does prejudice mean?

- How do you feel after reading the headlines?

- What evidence suggests that the headlines portray Muslims in a negative way?

- How can prejudice impact on emotional health?

Resources

- Headline news

Headline news

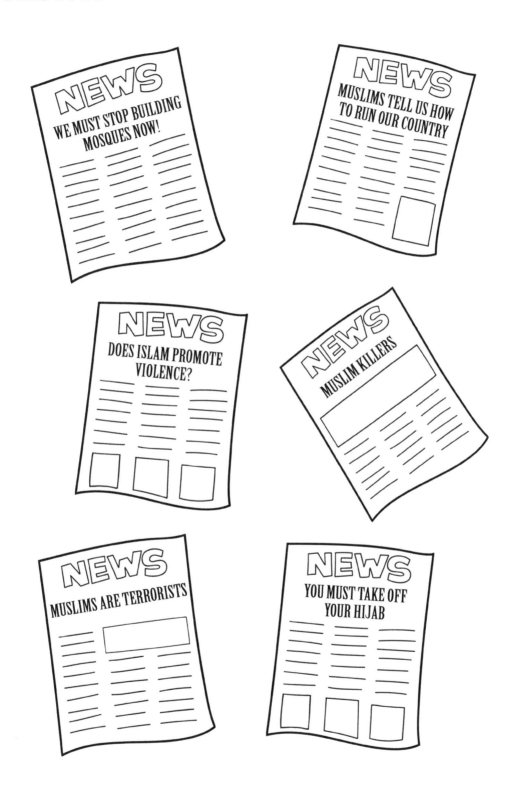

Activity 43

PSYCHOLOGICAL IMPACT OF ISLAMOPHOBIA (II)

Age: 9–11

Context

Prejudiced views are usually negative and are an unjustified attitude towards an individual or social group. It can cause division, and for children facing prejudice, the division can impact upon their relationships with others, lower self-esteem and cause self-doubt and isolation. Teaching children about community cohesion, kindness and respect can help them develop a greater understanding of individual differences.

Learning outcomes

The children will have an opportunity to:

- Reflect upon the definition of prejudice

- Reflect upon the definition of Islamophobia

- Recognise how their behaviours can affect others

- Explore feelings and emotions associated with prejudice

- Recognise factors that can influence thought and behaviour

- Find solutions for negative situations

Activity

This lesson can be used as a follow-up to Activity 42. Remind the children of the definition of prejudice and Islamophobia. Pose the questions: What do you remember about the words prejudice and Islamophobia? Where do prejudiced views come from and how do they affect others?

Tell the children that they are going to hear a story about a young girl called Nafisa who loves playing hockey. She enjoys training and playing in the matches with her teammates and has made great friends at her hockey club.

Read the story "Nafisa and her love for hockey" and ask the children to reflect and think about why she feels left out. Explore the impact of being treated unfairly as a result of individual difference related to race, religion and culture.

As an extension, invite the children to write the ending to the story using ideas discussed.

Questions for thinking

- What does Nafisa enjoy and how do you know?
- What evidence in the story suggests that she is feeling left out?
- Why does Nafisa feel left out of her hockey team?
- How is Nafisa feeling?
- What can Nafisa do about her situation?

Resources

- Nafisa and her love of hockey

Nafisa and her love for hockey

The ball flew into the top corner, sending the players wild. Nafisa raced over to join the celebrations, clutching her hijab as she burrowed into the huddle of screaming girls.

These were the moments Nafisa lived for. Although she didn't see any girls that looked like her in her team, she never felt that she was different. Her teammates were like a second family. To them, she was just Nafisa, and she loved how it made her feel.

The following day, Miss Lawrence, who coached the team, called a lunchtime meeting in the gym changing room.

"Girls," she said. "This is Jenny Taggart and Angela Burns." She gestured at two brown haired girls on the bench beside her. "They're your new teammates. So, let's make them welcome."

The two girls stood up slowly. Jenny was tall and muscular. Angela was shorter and a good deal heavier. Neither girl smiled.

"Okay, team," said Miss Lawrence once she'd finished her announcements. "Practice tomorrow at 4. Don't be late."

"What do you think of the newbies," said Nasifa's friend, Sarah, as they filed out of the gym. "A bit quiet weren't they."

"They're probably just nervous," said Nafisa. "I would be."

"Yeah, maybe," said Sarah. "Hope so."

At practice the next day, the team split into two groups. The new girls, Jenny and Angela, were in a group with Nafisa and Sarah. As they waited to start, Nafisa decided to say hello.

"Hi, I'm Nafisa," she said, offering her hand to Jenny.

"That right?" said Jenny, looking her up and down.

"And?" said Angela, with a smirk.

Before Nafisa could answer, Miss Lawrence blew the whistle, and the workout began.

"They're really good," said Sarah as she and Nafisa walked home after practice.

"Who?" said Nafisa quietly.

"The new girls. I mean, really good. And that Jen, she's such a laugh, Angela too. Everyone said so."

"I guess," said Nafisa.

That night, Nafisa lay in bed thinking. Why didn't the new girls like her? They seemed to like Sarah and the others okay. And what if her friends liked Jen and Angela better than her? Where would that leave her? Out in the cold? No, that couldn't happen. She loved her team, and she loved playing hockey. It wasn't fair. Nafisa felt really sad and started to question if it was because she looked different to them.

What was she going to do?

WHAT IS BLACK LIVES MATTER?

Age: 8–11

Context

The way in which children act, behave and respond will be influenced by what they see and hear. Teaching children about diversity, in particular racism, and the impact that it can have on mental health, should be integrated into school culture and education. The Black Lives Matter movement is one of many that illustrates the unfair treatment of Black people and the impact it can have on emotional health.

Learning outcomes

The children will have an opportunity to:

- Understand the definition of the Black Lives Matter movement

- Understand the definition of racism and diversity

- Identify the impact of racism on emotional health

- Illustrate compassion and develop empathy for others

- Find solutions for negative situations to create change

Activity

This activity will allow children to understand the reason for the Black Lives Matter movement and the importance of integration of equality. The activity will focus on the psychological impact of negative behaviours towards others and what they can do to help create integration.

Pose the question: What does diversity mean to you? Use this to lead onto the subject of racism. Explain that racism is treating someone unfairly because of their skin colour, nationality, culture and religious beliefs. Unfortunately, some people are treated unfairly because of these things which is why it is important to understand why this happens and what you can do to help.

Discuss that the Black Lives Matter movement is saying that racism is unacceptable and that everyone should be treated with fairness and given the same opportunities as everyone else. The movement is saddened that Black people are treated unfairly and believes that everyone should take responsibility in promoting kindness, respect and empathy. This will help towards creating equality and confident, resilient learners who will speak up when they know something is wrong.

Ask children to consider the impact that unjust treatment can have on emotional health. Invite them to research Black role-models or think of a Black person that they know. Ask them to create a positive affirmations poster using the "I am" resource that illustrates character strengths that this person embodies.

Questions for thinking

- What is the Black Lives Matter movement?

- What do diversity and racism mean?

- How does it make you feel when people are treated unfairly?

- What solutions could you provide for unjust treatment?

Resources

- I am

I am

Influencing Positive Change

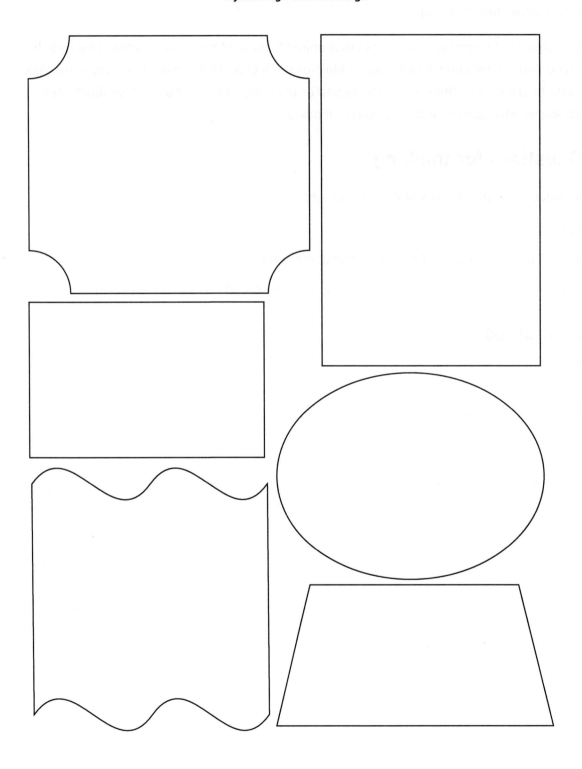

Activity 45

HOPE POWELL – BEING FIRST

Age: 8–11

Context

Hope Powell was the first Black woman to work as a national coach for the England Women's Football team and is considered a pioneer within the game. Hope was also the first woman to attain the UEFA Pro Licence – the highest qualification in the coaching education pathway. Hope has faced experiences of racism and sexism along her journey and has illustrated the character strengths of resilience and determination to help her achieve her goals.

Learning outcomes

The children will have an opportunity to:

- Learn about the life of Hope Powell

- Understand the challenges faced by Hope Powell

- Identify the impact of unfair treatment on emotional health

- Illustrate compassion and develop empathy for others

- Find solutions for negative situations to create change

Activity

This activity will teach children about Hope Powell, a Black role model, the challenges that she has faced and her pathway to success. Explain to the children that they are going to explore the life of a former professional footballer and coach, Hope Powell.

Read out the "Hope Powell" story and ask the children to think about the challenges that she faced and what helped her to overcome these challenges. Pose the question: How do you feel after hearing the story of Hope Powell? The discussion will allow children to demonstrate empathy as well as reflect upon the impact of discrimination as a result of individual difference.

Ask the children to analyse the information in the story as well as additional research, to create a fact sheet on Hope Powell using the "Being first" resource. Invite the children to share their work, considering the impact unfair treatment can have on emotional health.

Questions for thinking

- Who is Hope Powell?
- Can you identify some of the challenges that she has faced?
- How would you describe Hope Powell and why?
- What did she do to help her overcome her challenges?

Resources

- Hope Powell
- Being first

Hope Powell

At the age of 16, Hope Powell made her first England debut playing in the 1995 FIFA Women's World Cup – this was the first time the England Women's team had taken part in a World Cup tournament. Hope was vice-captain and stood tall and proud to have this role. A leader, not just in football, but in life. In 1998 she became the first Black female to coach the England Women's team – a decision that she questioned and a role that she thought she couldn't do.

As a Black female, Hope found it tough – she was challenged many times and would have to find ways to battle to prove herself over and over again. It was tiring and painful. Women's football didn't have very much money, so she would have to struggle – it was like a fight every day, asking for money to help her so that she could help the team.

Hope worked tirelessly, but felt burned out and at times, didn't feel that her work was being appreciated. It was a difficult job. She helped to develop several England Youth teams and was involved in coaching all of them, travelling all over the world – no other manager has ever done that.

Hope felt that she constantly needed to prove her knowledge, even though she had been a professional footballer, playing for England and Croydon, winning several trophies and medals in her career.

Sheer determination and resilience were needed, along with passion and a love for the game. The first woman to manage England and the first woman to achieve the Pro Licence, the highest coaching qualification.

In 2010 Hope Powell was awarded a CBE in the Queen's Birthday Honours list for her services to football.

Hope Powell is a pioneer and inspiration.

Being first

Activity 46

LEWIS LATIMER – INVENTOR AND PIONEER

Age: 8–11

Context

Lewis Howard Latimer was an African-American engineer and inventor who was a member of Thomas Edison's research team. The research team was known as Edison's Pioneers. Lewis Latimer improved the incandescent light bulb by inventing a carbon filament, which he patented in 1881. He also invented the threaded wooden socket for lightbulbs. Lewis Latimer is considered a pioneer and one of the most influential inventors of all time.

Learning outcomes

The children will have an opportunity to:

- Learn about the life of Lewis Latimer

- Identify the character strengths illustrated by Lewis Latimer

- Identify the impact of unfair treatment on emotional health

- Illustrate compassion and develop empathy for others

- Find solutions for negative situations to create change

Activity

This activity will teach children about Lewis Latimer, a Black role model and pioneer. The children will have the opportunity to learn about the character strengths that he illustrated to help him overcome challenges and adversity.

Explain to the children that they are going to explore the life of an inventor, Lewis Latimer who invented the carbon filament that is inside a lightbulb. Show children a lightbulb and use this to provoke thinking and questions.

Read out the "Lewis Latimer" story and ask the children to think about the challenges that he might have faced and the character strengths that he would have illustrated to help him manage these challenges. It is also important that children recognise that Lewis Latimer was one of the first Black inventors of all time and would have faced prejudice and discrimination in his life.

After reading the story, ask the children to reflect and analyse the information and list the character strengths that they think Lewis Latimer personified.

Questions for thinking

- Who was Lewis Latimer?

- What have you learned about his journey to becoming an inventor?

- Can you identify some of the challenges that he might have faced?

- Can you identify character strengths that Lewis Latimer would have used to help him overcome any challenges?

Resources

- Lewis Latimer

- Lewis Latimer – character strengths

Lewis Latimer

Lewis Latimer was an inventor and engineer best known for his contributions to creating and patenting the carbon filament in the light bulb.

A pioneer who is considered one of the most influential Black inventors of all time – his journey was not by any means easy. Lewis was born to parents who had fled slavery. An experience beyond anything that can be imagined – one of agony, cruelty and suffering. As runaway slaves, his father was captured by his slave owner, determined to take him back. Eventually, after a long ordeal of protests, his father was to be set free by supporters who were fighting to abolish slavery. Unfortunately, his father disappeared before the decision was reached, leaving Lewis to support his mother and family.

Growing up, Lewis served in the United States Navy during the Civil War and after being discharged from this post, he began to look for work. Working as an office assistant in a law patent firm formally introduced him to mechanical drawings. Lewis Latimer clearly had an innate passion and skill for mechanical drawing – practising and crafting by observing the work of an engineer that he worked with.

Things didn't always work out, but he would try over and over again. His focus and attention to detail showed that he wanted to learn. Lewis would spend hours learning the art of mechanical drawing. This was no easy task – it needed skill, patience and precision. These are technical drawings that help to show specific requirements and help to communicate problems and solutions that mechanical engineers may experience. The drawings are a big part of the planning process when creating an invention.

The firm recognised that Lewis was talented and promoted him soon after. Lewis went on to help others as well as create his own inventions, one being the carbon filament for the light bulb. Working with Thomas Edison's research team, known as the "Edison's Pioneers," Lewis found a way of improving the light bulb that was originally invented by Thomas Edison. Lewis found that although it did produce a glowing light, this light did not last very long.

He found a way of providing much longer life to the bulb by inventing the carbon filament which also made bulbs less expensive and more efficient. This helped electric lighting to be installed within homes and throughout streets.

Lewis Latimer became the leading light all over the world.

Lewis Latimer (character strengths)

PART X

RELATIONSHIPS

The resources in this section provide children with an opportunity to explore a range of relations including LGBTQ+ and the impact of prejudice and homophobia on emotional health.

Activity 47

MY IDENTITY

Age: 8–11

Context

A positive sense of identity for children is crucial to the development of self-esteem, confidence and belonging. A healthy sense of identity also teaches tolerance and helps children to be more open about themselves and to people from other backgrounds because they are less likely to fear differences or put other children down to feel better about themselves.

Learning outcomes

The children will have an opportunity to:

- Understand the definition of identity

- Recognise what identity means to them

- Recognise the impact of having a strong sense of identity on emotional health

- Understand the importance of tolerance and empathy

Activity

Explain to the children that they are going to be talking about their identities – things that make them who they are. Tell them that their identities can be described by their gender, culture, skin colour, religion and beliefs, hobbies and interests and anything that they think is important to them. Pose the question: How would you describe your identity? Help children to define any words that they may not be familiar with and explore themes that cover different aspects of diversity. This includes relationships, which is an important part of who they are. Children should not be afraid to talk about their heritage and should be provided with a safe environment that allows them to share with pride.

Tell the children that identity is created through storytelling, and these stories change throughout our lives as we live, learn and reflect on different experiences. Ask children to use the "My identity" resource to identify the things that make them who they are – this is an opportunity for the children to tell their story, through their eyes.

Questions for thinking

- What does identity mean to you?
- Can you name different types of relationships?
- What relationships are important to you and why?
- What do you understand by tolerance?
- What does tolerance teach us?
- How would you describe your identity?

Resources

- My identity

My identity

My name is_____

Activity 48

MY MUMS ARE GAY

Age: 9–11

Context

Teaching about relationships is an important part of educating children about our complex world. Learning about individual difference and the way in which people live their lives will enable children to develop respect and tolerance for those who are different from them. Focussing on family and friendships in all contexts will provide children with depth in knowledge and help them build the capacity to make informed choices about their wellbeing, health and relationships.

Learning outcomes

The children will have an opportunity to:

- Understand the definition of LGBTQ+
- Understand the definition of homophobia
- Recognise the impact of homophobia and bullying on emotional health
- Identify ways in which they can support others

Activity

When delivering relationship education, it is important that the needs of all children are appropriately met and that they understand the importance of equality and respect. The content and delivery should be sensitive and age appropriate. Teaching about LGBTQ+ should be integrated into the school programme to help eradicate any associated stigma and discrimination.

Before beginning the lesson, it is important that work has been done on understanding the acronym:

- Lesbian – a woman who is primarily attracted to women
- Gay – a man who is primarily attracted to men; sometimes a broad term used for individuals primarily attracted to the same sex
- Bi-sexual – an individual attracted to people of their own and other genders
- Transgender – a person whose gender or identity differs from their assigned sex at birth
- Queer – an umbrella term used by anyone in the LGBTQ+ community
- + – there are other queer identities not covered by the letters LGBTQ, for example a person may be asexual, non-binary or intersex, among many others

Use the poem "Do you know something I can do?" to provide children with an opportunity to openly discuss homophobia and the negative impact of bullying due to sexual orientation on emotional health.

Questions for thinking

- What does LQBTQ+ mean?
- What is homophobia?
- Why is the child being bullied?
- How is the child feeling and how do you know?
- What do you think the child should do?
- What would you do to help the child?

Resources

- Poem – Do you know something I can do?

Do you know something I can do?

So, here's the thing. My mums are gay.
There isn't any other way
to tell you how they think and feel.
So, there it is. Let's keep it real.

They stand together side by side,
support our family, taking pride
in who they are and what they give.
And that's the only way to live.

And as for me? Well, I don't mind.
They're just my parents,
sweet and kind.
They fell in love, and that's okay.
There shouldn't be a price to pay.

But at my school, some disagree.
And often take it out on me.
"Your mums are gay." They'll snigger and smile.
"I'm sure you must be one by looking at your style."

They laugh at me, and pull my hair,
and throw my homework everywhere
while saying stuff that's really mean,
"Don't sit with her. She isn't clean."

They always make sarcastic jokes.
"Hey, gather round. Now listen, folks.
She's got two mums. Oh, ain't that sad.
So, which is mum, and which is dad?"

My friends all do their best to say,
"Ignore them, and they'll go away.
They're bullies, stupid, full of hate.
We love your mums. They're really great."

I try to smile and jog along
like nothing in my world is wrong.
And, though they make me feel like dirt,
I kid myself it doesn't hurt.

But late at night, when I'm in bed,
I shed a tear for what they've said.
I just don't get the reason why
your parents must be girl and guy.

I've thought of telling mum and mum,
"These kids at school are total scum.
They haunt me like a witch's curse."
But that may only make it worse

Perhaps a teacher might be free,
to hear my tale of misery.
Or would they think I'm just a fool?
The tittle-tattler of the school.

Oh, I don't know. This isn't fun.
There should be room for everyone.
I love my parents just like you.
Do you know something I can do?

PART XI

DISABILITY

The resources in this section provide children with an opportunity to challenge stereotypes associated with disability using role models, including deaf awareness and the impact of unfair treatment on mental health.

Activity 49

DISABILITY DISCRIMINATION

Age: 8–11

Context

People with disability experience discrimination in all aspects of their life. Evidence suggests that people with learning disabilities are shown the greatest amount of stigma resulting in social exclusion, negatively impacting upon their mental health. Learning about the adversities that people with disability face will help to address stereotyping and challenge unconscious bias.

Learning outcomes

The children will have an opportunity to:

- Identify challenges faced by people with disabilities

- Challenge unconscious bias and stereotyping

- Discuss the impact of stereotyping and unconscious bias on others

- Recognise what can be put in place to ensure people with disabilities are included

Activity

Explain to the children that they are going to explore stigma and discrimination associated with people with disabilities. Ask the children to discuss the terms before providing a definition:

- Stigma is when a person is negatively labelled by an individual difference.

- Discrimination is treating someone unfairly because of an individual difference.

Provide examples to inform discussion:

- A wheelchair user is unable to attend a school of their choice because of the building

- An amputee is excluded by a group of children in the playground

Use the "Role model" resource cards to provide children with an opportunity to challenge stereotypes and discuss unconscious bias, thinking about how these thoughts are formed and what can be done to ensure people with disabilities are treated with fairness. It is also important that children recognise the negative impact of unfair treatment on emotional health.

Questions for thinking

- How could stereotyping have a negative impact on their mental and emotional health?
- What challenges do you think the individuals face?
- How do you think they have overcome these challenges?
- What characteristics have helped them to overcome the challenges?
- Has having a disability stopped them from achieving their goals and dreams?

Resources

- Role model cards

Role model cards

Kadeena Cox is a Parasport athlete.
She has multiple sclerosis. This means that her muscles may become stiff and she could get extremely tired. In the 2016 Paralympic Games she became the first British Paralympian to win Gold medals in multiple sports at the same games, since Isabel Barr in 1984.

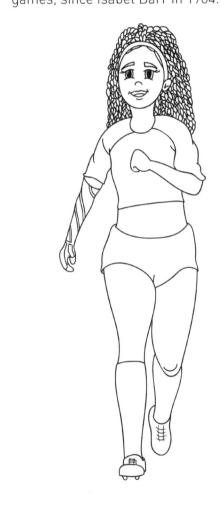

Sudha Chandran is an extremely talented Indian dancer and actress. Following an accident, she had her right leg amputated and was given an artificial leg. She found this to be the toughest part of her life but was determined to regain mobility and get back to dancing. She has received many awards and has been invited to all parts of the world to provide inspiration to many disabled people who aspire to dance.

Ade Adepitan is a British television presenter and a wheelchair basketball player. He uses a wheelchair as a result of developing polio as a child which led to loss of use of his left leg. At the age of 3, he emigrated to England from Lagos, Nigeria. Ade has represented Team GB in wheelchair basketball and won Gold in the 2005 Paralympic World Cup. Ade does a lot of charity work helping other people with physical disabilities.

Ellie Simmonds is a Paralympian swimmer. She has achondroplasia which is a common cause of dwarfism. In the 2008 Summer Paralympics she won two Gold medals for Team GB, despite being the youngest member of the team, only aged 13. In the 2012 Olympics, she won another 2 Gold medals and set the World record in 400m freestyle. This success was continued in the Rio Olympics, 2016.

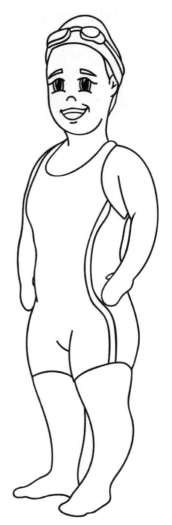

Sadhna Dhand suffered from brittle bone disease and lost all her hearing at 12 years old. Her bone disease makes her bones fragile and affects her growth. As a result, she only stands 3' 3 inches tall. She has won national awards for her painting skills and helps charities who work with disabled children.

Stephen Hawking was a theoretical physicist and cosmologist interested in physics and the origins of the universe. At the age of 21, he was diagnosed with multi-neurone disease and was given only 2 more years to live. He lived until he was 76 years old. He had been paralysed from head to toe for over 30 years and used a wheelchair and a voice synthesiser to be able to communicate. He became well known for his work as a researcher and professor gaining awards all over the world.

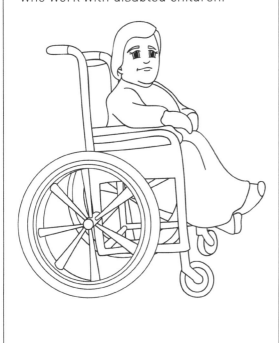

Activity 50

IMAGINE MY WORLD

Age: 8–11

Context

Children should learn that disability discrimination is when someone is treated less well or put at a disadvantage for a reason that relates to their disability. It is also important that children are aware that not all disabilities are visible. Conditions such as psychotic mental health disorders, epilepsy, attention-deficit/hyperactivity disorder (ADHD) or certain learning disorders are common hidden disabilities that might not be so obvious. Championing deaf awareness helps children to develop empathy and better understanding of others.

Learning outcomes

The children will have an opportunity to:

- Identify challenges faced by people with hearing loss

- Challenge unconscious bias and stereotyping

- Discuss the emotional impact of unfair treatment on people who are deaf

- Recognise what can be put in place to ensure people who are deaf are included

- Identify ways in which they can promote deaf awareness in their school

Activity

Explain to the children that they will be exploring unfair treatment towards people who are deaf. Tell them that according to the charity, Action Hearing Loss, one in six people are deaf or have hearing loss; therefore they are likely to meet someone who is deaf or has some level of hearing loss.

Pose the questions: Do you know someone or have any friends who are deaf? How do you communicate with them? Lead this onto discussing the type of discrimination that people who are deaf could face and why. 12 million in the UK are affected and they all face communication challenges resulting in loneliness or frustration.

Use the poem "Imagine my world" to engage the children in discussion on the impact of discrimination on emotional health because of ignorance on deafness, and strategies that can be used to communicate with people who are deaf or have hearing loss. These might include:

- Face the person and speak clearly
- Avoid speaking too fast or shouting
- Use simple gestures such as pointing
- Write things down on a piece of paper

Questions for thinking

- How do you feel after hearing the poem?
- How is the character in the poem feeling?
- Why do you think he feels this way?
- What can he do to help him find a solution for overcoming his situation?
- What can you do to help promote deaf awareness in your school?

Resources

- Poem – Imagine my world

Imagine my world

Imagine my world.
It's quieter than yours,
in playgrounds and classrooms,
at home and in stores.

The noise of the traffic,
the things people say,
the music and laughter
are so far away.

I can't hear you coming.
I can't hear you go.
If I don't see you moving
I just wouldn't know.

My hearing aid helps.
But it isn't a cure.
I'm deaf, and I know it,
and that is for sure.

I'm learning to lip read,
and trying to sign.
But like any new language,
it's taking some time.

And talking is hard
as confusion surrounds
how to form all the words
when you can't hear the sounds.

But just cos I'm deaf
doesn't mean that I'm odd.
Every kid on the Earth
is the same before God.

Though I may not hear much,
there's a lot I can feel.
When you punish my deafness,
the hurting is real.

When you shout in my ears
or you laugh in my face,
when you whisper and point,
it's a total disgrace.

When you try to make fun
of the way that I speak.
When you kick me and pinch me
and call me a freak.

When I can't understand.
When I seem a bit lost.
When I ask for your help,
but you don't give a toss.

When I'm sat in my chair,
and you think it's alright
to just sneak up behind me
and give me a fright.

These things are all hurtful.
I'm not made of stone.
You don't have to like me,
but leave me alone.

Cos I'm deaf, and that's sad,
but it's not a disease.
I can go where I want to
and do what I please.

I can be anything
that I dream I can be.
So, okay, I can't hear.
But I'm free to be me.

For Product Safety Concerns and Information please contact
our EU representative GPSR@taylorandfrancis.com Taylor & Francis
Verlag GmbH, Kaufingerstraße 24, 80331 München, Germany

T - #0085 - 090625 - C0 - 297/210/10 - SB - 9780367708252 - Gloss Lamination